# facebook
## and Your Marriage

# facebook
## and Your Marriage

K. Jason & Kelli Krafsky

Turn the Tide

# facebook
## and Your Marriage

**Facebook and Your Marriage**
K. Jason & Kelli Krafsky
Copyright © 2010 by K. Jason & Kelli Krafsky

Printed and bound in the United States of America. All rights reserved. No part of this book may be reproduced in any form or by any electronic or mechanical means including photocopying, recording, or any other information storage and retrieval systems without permission in writing by the publisher, except by a reviewer or journalist, who may quote brief passages in a print or online review, article or column.

Published by **Turn the Tide Resource Group, LLC**, 26828 Maple Valley Hwy #260, Maple Valley, Washington 98038. T3RG@ FullMarriageExperience.com. 425.432.TIDE (8433).

Although the author and publisher have made every effort to ensure the accuracy and completeness of information contained in this book, we assume no responsibility for errors, inaccuracies, omissions, or any inconsistency herein. Any slights of people, places, or organizations are unintended. Readers should use their judgment and consult clergy, professional counselor, or specialized relationship educator for more intensive relationship issues.

First printing 2010

**Find us on the web: FacebookAndYourMarriage.com.**
**Find us on Facebook: facebook.com/FBandYourMarriage**
**Find us on Twitter: twitter.com/FB_and_Marriage**

ISBN 9780976955610

ATTENTION CHURCHES, COMMUNITY INITIATIVES, CORPORATIONS, COUNSELING AGENCIES, BOOKSTORES, NON-PROFIT ORGANIZATIONS: Quantity discounts are available on bulk purchases of this book for educational, gift giving, or fundraising purposes.

For special orders, please contact **Turn the Tide Resource Group, LLC**, 26828 Maple Valley Hwy #260, Maple Valley, Washington 98038 info@FBMarriage.com 425.432.TIDE (8433).

Project Editor: K. Jason Krafsky

Copy Editor: Michael Umlandt

Proofreader: Lori Dilio

Artistic direction, design and photography by Michelle De Monnin for DeMonnin's Art Studio, www.demonnin.com

Additional photography and images provided by DesignPics, istockphoto and Jessica Christine Photography, jcgawwaway.snappages.com

Printing: PrintNW

Special thanks to all those who donated profile photos

Production coordinated by Turn the Tide Resource Group, LLC

**Turn the Tide**
resource group

# Dedication

**Jason & Kelli:**

We dedicate Facebook and Your Marriage to our four amazing kids — Caleb, Jaelyn, Josh and Cole! We love you very much!!!

**Caleb:**

Since our names are used in the first few pages of the book and we didn't sign a waiver, do we get a royalty for every book sold? Ha Ha!

**Jaelyn:**

Wait! Who are the people on the front cover? Oh…it's you guys! I get it now. LOL

**Josh:**

Thanks Mom and Dad! Didn't say much about us tho. How about Josh is our third child who is funny, charming, nice on the eyes, and a good soccer player?

▶▶▶

**Cole:**

Can I play the Wii?

---

**Jason & Kelli:**

We would like to undedicate this book to our kids. ☺

---

**Krafsky Kids:**

Us amazing kids think this is pretty cool! Woohoo Mom and Dad!

# Acknowledgements
## (Special Shout Out)

*Facebook and Your Marriage* was simply an idea in early 2009. It moved from concept to book a year later because of a whole bunch of people.

When we posted the blog articles ("Is Facebook a Cyber-Threat to Your Marriage?" and "How Facebook Can Improve Your Marriage") on MarriageJunkie.com, some people we knew and a lot we didn't sent private messages and posted comments on how helpful and needed the information was. A lot of people linked it, reposted it, referred to it, tweeted it, and emailed it on to others. Your input and encouragement made us see that many spouses have a tremendous need for a resource like *Facebook and Your Marriage*. Thanks to all of you!

After outlining the book, we floated the concept of *Facebook and Your Marriage* to a number of friends and colleagues, most especially Dr. Matthew Turvey of Life Innovations, Dr. Michael Sytsma of the Institute for Sexual Wholeness, JoAnn Kraft, a marriage and family therapist, and Eric and Jennifer Garcia of the Association of Marriage and Family Ministries (AMFM). These are the kinds of friends who will really tell you if an idea is good or if it isn't. They all strongly advocated that this book needed to be written. Thank you for the invaluable input and insights that helped us take the idea to a whole new level.

As we wrote the manuscript, we leaned on a myriad of incredible, marriage-strengthening resources produced by organizations and individuals who are passionate about improving the quality and health of relationships: Smart Marriages, California Healthy Marriages Coalition, AMFM, Dave Carder, Michele Weiner-Davis, the late Shirley Glass, PREP, and many, many more that are referenced and linked at **FacebookAndYourMarriage.com**. Our own marriage as well as our efforts to strengthen other people's marriages is better because of your wisdom, insights, and relationship tools.

As the manuscript neared completion, a talented team was assembled to move the words from a Word document to an actual book. Michelle De Monnin of De Monnin's Art Studio went above and beyond the call of duty and blew us away with a cover design and inside design that is beyond perfect! Bradley Burck of Burck Communications lined us up with a talented copy editor, Mike Umlandt, and a gifted web designer, Nathanael Merrill of Merrill Interactive. Our proofreader, Lori Dilio, has a natural eye for typos, misspellings, and grammatical errors. This book is what it is because of each of you! And thanks to Duane Montague for providing some creative promo copy.

Ultimately, we want to thank Facebook. You have created an amazing technology allowing us to stay connected with a lot more people than should be humanly possible. And Facebook wouldn't be what it is without our FB Friends (and now fans of *Facebook and Your Marriage*) who have made the Facebook experience memorable, fun, and worth writing about. You all have helped us in writing this more than you know!

See you on Facebook! —*Jason & Kelli*

# Preface

**Facebook has forever changed how we do things on the web.**

It has a worldwide membership that well exceeds the total population of the United States. Those members access Facebook multiple times every day on their computers, laptops and mobile phones. Facebook has broken through the barriers of who we have access to and how we interact with them.

The evidence that Facebook is the most popular social gathering place on the planet is that the term "Facebook" no longer just refers to a social network site. The word is used in a variety of ways to describe a form of communication ("Why don't you facebook me later."), an activity ("We're just facebooking with our friends."), and an identity ("Hello, my fellow Facebookers.")

It seems that most of what Facebook offers is positive. Athletes, musicians and celebrities use Facebook to interact with fans and grow their fan support. Non-profits use Facebook to raise money and build awareness of their causes. Businesses use Facebook to reach new customers and maintain customer loyalty with old ones. Churches use Facebook for outreach and building community with their congregation.

Everyone seems to be benefiting by leveraging Facebook in a good and purposeful way. Except for one large demographic group...married people.

Think about it. The only real negative stories about Facebook highlight the affect it is having on marriages. There was the "first Facebook divorce" story, countless accounts of emotional affairs, infidelity, and broken marriages due to a spouse finding an old flame on Facebook, and now, the largely overstated "1 in 5 divorces caused by Facebook" articles.

We made this observation in late 2008...almost every negative story about Facebook had to do with infidelity, divorce and broken families.

So we wrote a couple of blog articles to provide married Facebookers with tips on how to protect their marriage while on Facebook, and improve their relationship using Facebook. The articles were posted on MarriageJunkie.com (Jason's blog) and the response was overwhelmingly positive. (To this day, they are still the most popular posts on the blog.)

Through comments on the blog, direct emails, messages on Facebook and face-to-face conversations, married people expressed they wanted and needed more information on this topic. Wives and husbands have shared with us heart-breaking stories of betrayal and pain. Most innocently jumped into Facebook with the greatest of intentions, and found themselves with a broken heart and a broken marriage.

As we discussed the reactions and responses to the articles, we discovered that many people were blindsided by how easy

▶▶▶

it was to connect with people from the past, and they were unprepared to handle those reconnections.

We observed that most of the couples hadn't set guardrails on their time and relationships on Facebook. Combined with a lack of some common sense (by one or both partners), trouble ensued. And once a boundary was crossed, many were at a loss of what to do about it.

Somehow, couples need to be better informed about what can happen on Facebook and how to proactively protect their marriage. Something needs to guide spouses on how to use Facebook to build a stronger marriage, how to handle tough situations from time spent on Facebook, how to identify where the "old" feelings sparked by Facebook are coming from, and how to effectively work through any relationship issues related to Facebook. Someone needs to put this information into a book.

That someone is us. That something is *Facebook and Your Marriage*. That somehow is you reading this book.

With *Facebook and Your Marriage*, it is our hope to bring common sense and healthy boundaries back into marriages in this social media age.

—K. Jason & Kelli Krafsky

# HEY! READ THIS BEFORE STARTING!

**Do not treat this book like a regular book!**

*Facebook and Your Marriage* meets you where you are and directs you to the answers you're looking for...and more! Whether you've just created your profile or you're a veteran user, *Facebook and Your Marriage,* in an easy to use format, will help you quickly find answers to more than 120 common questions people have about Facebook.

**Do not think of this book like a regular cover-to-cover read!**

*Facebook and Your Marriage*'s layout resembles a thread one would see on an online blog or discussion board. A thread is an online discussion on a central topic between two or more people. We have taken the layout and approach of threads and put them into book form. The threads are based on real questions from married (and in some cases, unmarried) Facebookers.

**Do not start with the first page of the first section!**

Your issues and needs are different from someone else's. Are you a novice or an advanced Facebook user? The needs of users are different. Is yours, or your spouse's Facebook experience having no real affect on your marriage, a huge impact on the marriage, or somewhere in between? Because the issues are

▶▶▶

different, the answers are different. Your starting point is going to be different than someone else's.

While most books have a table of contents, this book has Discussion Thread Topics. These pages list ten primary sections with over 120 threads. Find the topics that most interest you and start there.

**Do not just read one thread and stop!**

A single thread is intended to be a sum part of the whole answer you need. It answers one question. At the end of each thread is a list of five Related Threads that will help you unpack more of the issue and get a deeper answer to your questions. Just like on a website, you are in total control of finding the answers that will satisfy your unique needs and wants. Sometimes you will know where you need to go. Other times, the book will take you on a journey to discover answers to issues you didn't even know you had.

**Do not presume that all your questions on Facebook are answered in this book!**

By no means is this book intended to be an exhaustive manual on everything a person can do on Facebook. Those books have been written. With the title, *Facebook and Your Marriage*, there should be no mystery on the types of topics this book addresses. Because Facebook regularly undergoes changes to its layouts and features, the specific Facebook how-to's are found on FacebookAndYourMarriage.com. They range from short articles to visual instructions to help you get the most out of Facebook.

▶▶▶

**Do not assume that the authors are counselors or marriage therapists!**

*Facebook and Your Marriage* is not a book by professional counselors. It's written by a married couple who actually use Facebook every day. We have learned through trial-and-error how to protect our marriage, enhance our marriage, and even use Facebook to grow closer as a couple.

We are active on Facebook and even more active to make our marriage as strong and healthy as it can be. For almost our entire married life (which started in 1994), we have been premarital and marriage educators and involved in a national movement to foster healthy couple relationships...before and after the wedding day. And now, online and offline.

# Discussion Thread Topics

# Discussion Thread Topics

Section 1

## Facebook 411: Making Sense of Facebook

*Facebook has a language and culture all its own that breeds a lot of questions by beginners getting their feet wet and observers on the sidelines of the world's largest online social community. Get your answers on the basics in this set of threads!*

- ▸ Facebook in a Nutshell........................30
- ▸ Facebook's Conception, Birth & First Steps...........32
- ▸ Your BFF — Bonafide Facebook Friend ............34
- ▸ Comparing Online Social Networks...............36
- ▸ Facebook Special Features...................38
- ▸ Can a Guy Get Some Privacy?.................40
- ▸ The Profile Page ........................42
- ▸ Home Sweet Home (Page) ..................44
- ▸ Updating Your Status.....................47
- ▸ The Wall..............................50
- ▸ Making Sense of the News Feed................52
- ▸ A Knock-Off on Real Relationships?..............54
- ▸ Fad or Fixture?.........................56
- ▸ Is Facebook Evil?........................58
- ▸ Should Married Facebookers Beware? ...........60
- ▸ Your Own Paparazzi…Sort Of ................63

**facebook** *and Your Marriage*

# Discussion Thread Topics

Section 2

## C'mon! Join the Rest of the Planet on Facebook

Hundreds of millions of people have taken the plunge and joined Facebook. When first getting started, they all wrestled with many of the issues dealt with in this series of threads. Find beneficial answers to questions you may not even know you have (yet).

- ▶ Joint or Solo Account?.............................68
- ▶ Starting Up on Facebook..........................70
- ▶ Maiden or Married Name?........................72
- ▶ Your Profile Picture.................................74
- ▶ Relationship Status.................................76
- ▶ Info About Me........................................78
- ▶ Finding Friends......................................80
- ▶ Friend Swap with Spouse?........................82
- ▶ Handling Friend Requests.........................84
- ▶ Find-A-Friend Suggestions........................86
- ▶ The Right Amount of Updates...................88
- ▶ Your Friends Are Hot (Linked)!..................90
- ▶ Posting & Commenting Etiquette...............92
- ▶ Facebook Email......................................94
- ▶ About the Chat Feature...........................96
- ▶ A Note About Notes................................98
- ▶ All the Fun Stuff...Applications................100
- ▶ Joining Groups & Pages..........................102

facebook
and Your Marriage

# Discussion Thread Topics

Section 3

## Let's Go! Take Your FB Experience to the Next Level

*You've been a part of the social network long enough to see things that you don't know how to do or make a part of your Facebook experience. Learn how to tap Facebook for all it's worth and move from novice to expert in no time flat.*

- ▶ Custom Facebook URL . . . . . . . . . . . . . . . . . . . . . . . . . . . 108
- ▶ SOS for Lost Friends . . . . . . . . . . . . . . . . . . . . . . . . . . . . .110
- ▶ Creating Friend Lists . . . . . . . . . . . . . . . . . . . . . . . . . . . . .112
- ▶ Making Web Links Work . . . . . . . . . . . . . . . . . . . . . . . . . .114
- ▶ Sharing Pictures . . . . . . . . . . . . . . . . . . . . . . . . . . . . . . . .116
- ▶ Declining Friend Requests with Dignity . . . . . . . . . . . . .118
- ▶ Handling Serial Facebookers . . . . . . . . . . . . . . . . . . . . . .121
- ▶ What the @ Is This? . . . . . . . . . . . . . . . . . . . . . . . . . . . . 124
- ▶ Dealing with Flirts . . . . . . . . . . . . . . . . . . . . . . . . . . . . . . 126
- ▶ Quiz & Game Notifications . . . . . . . . . . . . . . . . . . . . . . 128
- ▶ Linking Your Phone & Facebook . . . . . . . . . . . . . . . . . . 130
- ▶ Tweeting Facebook, Facebooking Twitter . . . . . . . . . . . 132
- ▶ Starting a (Facebook) Family (Group) . . . . . . . . . . . . . . 136
- ▶ R.I.P. My Facebook Friend . . . . . . . . . . . . . . . . . . . . . . . 138

facebook and Your Marriage

# Discussion Thread Topics

Section 4

## K.I.S.S. — Simple Ways to Safeguard Your Marriage, Your Spouse, and Yourself

*Facebook doesn't cause marriage problems, people do. This thread set shares practical tips and ideas to help spouses avoid many of the problem areas and awkward situations some married people can find themselves in on Facebook.*

- ▶ The R.D.A. for Facebook . . . . . . . . . . . . . . . . . . . . . . . . . . 142
- ▶ Responding to Friends . . . . . . . . . . . . . . . . . . . . . . . . . . . 144
- ▶ Password Exchange . . . . . . . . . . . . . . . . . . . . . . . . . . . . . 146
- ▶ Avoiding FB Addiction . . . . . . . . . . . . . . . . . . . . . . . . . . . 148
- ▶ Let Facebook Know You're Married . . . . . . . . . . . . . . . . . 150
- ▶ Safeguards with Non-FB Spouse . . . . . . . . . . . . . . . . . . . 152
- ▶ Talking FB with Non-FB Spouse . . . . . . . . . . . . . . . . . . . . 154
- ▶ Following the Golden Rule . . . . . . . . . . . . . . . . . . . . . . . . 156
- ▶ Finding Mutual Friends . . . . . . . . . . . . . . . . . . . . . . . . . . . 158
- ▶ Offensive Facebook Ads . . . . . . . . . . . . . . . . . . . . . . . . . . 160
- ▶ Chatting Boundaries . . . . . . . . . . . . . . . . . . . . . . . . . . . . . 162
- ▶ Friending Exes...or Not? . . . . . . . . . . . . . . . . . . . . . . . . . . 164
- ▶ Friending an Ex-Spouse . . . . . . . . . . . . . . . . . . . . . . . . . . 167
- ▶ Handling Embarrassing Comments . . . . . . . . . . . . . . . . . 170

facebook and Your Marriage

# Discussion Thread Topics

Section 5

## Surprise! How to Expect the Unexpected and Not Sweat It

*The biggest challenge of being a part of the world's largest subculture is not knowing how to handle unpredictable situations and unexpected correspondences. Get the inside scoop on how to expect the unexpected and what to do when it occurs (and it will).*

- ▶ Getting Poked .................................................. 174
- ▶ Chat Responses ................................................ 176
- ▶ Friend Requests from Old Flames ................. 179
- ▶ International Friend Requests....................... 182
- ▶ Comments — Choose Peace Not War ............ 184
- ▶ When Private Stuff Goes Public .................... 186
- ▶ Removing Bad Photos .................................... 188
- ▶ Hiding, Removing & Blocking People ............191
- ▶ Something Seems Phishy............................... 194
- ▶ Is Message Legit or a Scam? ......................... 196
- ▶ Reducing Activities Reporting ...................... 198
- ▶ Closing Facebook Account ............................200

**facebook**
and Your Marriage

# Discussion Thread Topics

Section 6

## Let's Get It On! Have a Facebook Affair… With Your Spouse!

*Spouses have a new tool in their cache to romance their loved one…Facebook. This set of threads is filled with flirty ideas and romantic suggestions to utilize Facebook as another way to express love to one's mate and regularly woo your spouse.*

- Loving a Non-FB Spouse on Facebook . . . . . . . . . . . . . . 204
- Sharing the Love Through Updates . . . . . . . . . . . . . . . . 208
- Flirting on Facebook . . . . . . . . . . . . . . . . . . . . . . . . . . . . 210
- Show `Em More Love . . . . . . . . . . . . . . . . . . . . . . . . . . . 212
- Go on Facebook Dates . . . . . . . . . . . . . . . . . . . . . . . . . . 214
- Posting Poems & Love Notes . . . . . . . . . . . . . . . . . . . . . 217
- Be Long Distance Lovers . . . . . . . . . . . . . . . . . . . . . . . . 220
- Special Moment Shout-Outs . . . . . . . . . . . . . . . . . . . . . 222
- Creative Invites to Date Your Mate . . . . . . . . . . . . . . . . 224
- The Ultimate Surprise . . . . . . . . . . . . . . . . . . . . . . . . . . 226

**facebook** *and Your Marriage*

# Discussion Thread Topics

Section 7

## SOS! My Marriage Is Suffering Because of Facebook!

*What happens on Facebook does not stay on Facebook. And when married people do questionable things on Facebook, it can negatively impact their marriage. This thread series is intended to help spouses figure out how to handle a difficult situation when their Facebooking spouse has made poor choices and bad decisions on Facebook.*

- Spouse Spends Too Much Time on FB . . . . . . . . . . . . . . . . 232
- Mate Is Chronic Updater. . . . . . . . . . . . . . . . . . . . . . . . . . . 235
- Having Insecurity Surges . . . . . . . . . . . . . . . . . . . . . . . . . . 238
- Concerns with Spouse Friending Exes . . . . . . . . . . . . . . . . 242
- Spouse Broke Agreement on Friends . . . . . . . . . . . . . . . . . 245
- Viewing Spouse's Chat Sessions . . . . . . . . . . . . . . . . . . . . 248
- Logging Into My Mate's Facebook . . . . . . . . . . . . . . . . . . . 251
- Is It an Emotional Affair? . . . . . . . . . . . . . . . . . . . . . . . . . . 254
- Caught Spouse but I'm to Blame? . . . . . . . . . . . . . . . . . . . 257
- Confronting Spouse About Affair . . . . . . . . . . . . . . . . . . . . 260
- Spouse Changes "Married" to "It's Complicated" . . . . . 264
- Ex-Spouse OK as FB Friend? . . . . . . . . . . . . . . . . . . . . . . . 268
- Is Our Marriage Over? . . . . . . . . . . . . . . . . . . . . . . . . . . . . 271
- Spouse Wants a Do-Over . . . . . . . . . . . . . . . . . . . . . . . . . . 274

# Discussion Thread Topics

Section 8

## Seriously? Let's Think This Through a Bit More

*Reconnecting with people from one's past can be a fun and thrilling experience. Problem? Some reconnections are not good for one's marriage. This thread is intended to help Facebookers sort through their feelings and emotions as well as their choices and actions before, during, or after making marriage-threatening decisions.*

- ▶ Make Past Boy/Girlfriend a Current FB Friend?........280
- ▶ Ex's Profile Pic Sparks Feelings .....................282
- ▶ Spouse Overreacting on Friend Choices..............284
- ▶ Can't Wait to Facebook with Someone...............286
- ▶ Changing My Status to "It's Complicated"...........288
- ▶ My Spouse Is Spying on Me........................291
- ▶ Rekindled Romance on Facebook ...................294
- ▶ From Facebook to Face-to-Face ....................298
- ▶ Am I About to Have an Affair? .....................301
- ▶ Leaving My Marriage..............................304
- ▶ Repairing a Marriage I Messed Up ..................308

facebook
and Your Marriage

# Discussion Thread Topics

Section 9

## TMI! Talking with Your Mate Offline About Online Issues

*Facebook is a part of our lives. Therefore, it is a part of our marriage life too. Facebook is something all couples should talk about...in real time. This thread set gives couples everything they need to make their conversations and conflicts as stress-free and solution-based as possible using communication tools and skills guaranteed to make their time on Facebook safer and their marriage stronger.*

- ▶ Talking Without Fighting . . . . . . . . . . . . . . . . . . . . . . . . . . 314
- ▶ Setting Up Boundaries . . . . . . . . . . . . . . . . . . . . . . . . . . . . 319
- ▶ Resolving Conflict Quickly . . . . . . . . . . . . . . . . . . . . . . . . . 322
- ▶ Turning Screaming Matches Into Conversations . . . . . . 325
- ▶ Finding Solutions for Your FB Problems . . . . . . . . . . . . . 328
- ▶ Uh-Huh Is Never Enough . . . . . . . . . . . . . . . . . . . . . . . . . 331
- ▶ The "About Us" Date . . . . . . . . . . . . . . . . . . . . . . . . . . . . 334
- ▶ Calling for an "About Us" Date . . . . . . . . . . . . . . . . . . . . 338
- ▶ Creating Your Own Boundaries . . . . . . . . . . . . . . . . . . . . 341
- ▶ Living Inbounds . . . . . . . . . . . . . . . . . . . . . . . . . . . . . . . . .344
- ▶ Working Through Infidelity Together . . . . . . . . . . . . . . .346
- ▶ Finding Help . . . . . . . . . . . . . . . . . . . . . . . . . . . . . . . . . . . 349

**facebook** and Your Marriage

# Discussion Thread Topics

## Back of the Book Stuff

- Appendix A: Get More from
  *Facebook and Your Marriage* Online . . . . . . . . . . . . . . . . 354
- Appendix B: Facebook Jargon . . . . . . . . . . . . . . . . . . . . . 356
- Appendix C: Sources. . . . . . . . . . . . . . . . . . . . . . . . . . . . . 360
- About the Authors: K. Jason & Kelli Krafsky . . . . . . . . 364
- Other Books by K. Jason & Kelli Krafsky . . . . . . . . . . . . 366
- Order More Copies of
  *Facebook and Your Marriage* . . . . . . . . . . . . . . . . . . . . . 370

## Section 1

*Facebook has a language and culture all its own that breeds a lot of questions by beginners getting their feet wet and observers on the sidelines of the world's largest online social community. Get your answers on the basics in this set of threads!*

- ▶ Facebook in a Nutshell .................................. 30
- ▶ Facebook's Conception, Birth & First Steps ............. 32
- ▶ Your BFF — Bonafide Facebook Friend .................. 34
- ▶ Comparing Online Social Networks ..................... 36
- ▶ Facebook Special Features ............................. 38
- ▶ Can a Guy Get Some Privacy? .......................... 40
- ▶ The Profile Page ....................................... 42
- ▶ Home Sweet Home (Page) ............................... 44
- ▶ Updating Your Status .................................. 47
- ▶ The Wall .............................................. 50
- ▶ Making Sense of the News Feed ........................ 52
- ▶ A Knock-Off on Real Relationships? .................... 54
- ▶ Fad or Fixture? ........................................ 56
- ▶ Is Facebook Evil? ...................................... 58
- ▶ Should Married Facebookers Beware? ................... 60
- ▶ Your Own Paparazzi...Sort Of ......................... 63

# Facebook 411: Making Sense of Facebook

# Facebook in a Nutshell

Facebook 411: Making Sense of Facebook

## Facebook Jargon

Facebook is an online community that allows people to connect and reconnect with old and new friends, family members, former classmates, and just about anybody else.

**I'm trying to tell a friend about Facebook. How do you explain Facebook to someone who's never been on it?**

### Jason & Kelli:

Imagine a never-ending, ever-evolving gathering of family, friends, and acquaintances from your past, present, and future. That's Facebook.

Facebook is an online community that allows people to connect and reconnect with old and new friends, family members, former classmates, and just about anybody else (Facebook calls them friends, and from here on we'll refer to them as FB Friends). The brilliance of Facebook is that you can connect with more people from your past and present than you ever could by making phone calls, sending emails, and mailing letters combined.

### Jason:

With a fraction of the time and energy.

### Jason & Kelli:

On Facebook, you share what's going on in your life. In real-time, your updates show up on all of your FB Friends' Home Pages where they can read it, react to it, comment on it, or ignore it.

▶▶▶

**facebook** *and Your Marriage*

30

# Facebook 411: Making Sense of Facebook

# Facebook in a Nutshell

And at the same time, your Home Page will show the latest updates by your FB Friends.

In addition to viewing what their FB Friends are doing, people share photos and videos, send links and articles, play games, join different Groups, become fans of different Pages, send emails, and chat with each other through Facebook.

**Kelli:**

To me, Facebook is more than just a website. It is a part of my daily routine to stay in contact and keep up with people I care about.

## Our Book Club Picks

*Facebook For Dummies, 2nd Edition* Authored by two Facebook employees who provide unique insight and insider knowledge of Facebook that can't be found anywhere else.

## Related Threads:

- ▶ Your BFF — Bonafide Facebook Friend . . . . . . . . . 34
- ▶ Comparing Online Social Networks . . . . . . . . . . . . 36
- ▶ Home Sweet Home (Page) . . . . . . . . . . . . . . . . . . . . 44
- ▶ The Profile Page . . . . . . . . . . . . . . . . . . . . . . . . . . . 42
- ▶ Starting Up on Facebook . . . . . . . . . . . . . . . . . . . . 70

**facebook** and Your Marriage

31

# Facebook's Conception, Birth & First Steps

Facebook 411: Making Sense of Facebook

## Numbers Don't Lie

Facebook 100-Million Milestones

August 2008: 100 million users

April 2009: 200 million users

September 2009: 300 million users

February 2010: 400 million users

### How did Facebook get started?

**Jason & Kelli:**

You've heard those stories of how a guy creates something in college, drops out of college, and makes gazillions of dollars?

**Jason:**

Yeah, that's Facebook's storyline too.

**Jason & Kelli:**

In 2004, Mark Zuckerberg was attending Harvard when he and a few other students (Dustin Moskovitz, Chris Hughes, and Eduardo Saverin) developed The Facebook (the original name of the networking site) as a way for classmates at the Ivy League school to stay connected. With some financial help, the social network was expanded to Stanford and Yale, and soon thereafter, colleges across the nation.

Zuckerberg and Moskovitz dropped out of school to focus on their emerging business venture. In August 2005, the name of the site was officially changed to Facebook.

▶▶▶

facebook
and Your Marriage

# Facebook's Conception, Birth & First Steps

As the network expanded, more and more people were invited into the online community; any college student, then high schoolers, and in 2006 the doors to Facebook were opened to everyone over the age of thirteen.

Facebook is now used by celebrities and the common, business leaders and the unemployed, the famous and the unknown.

**Kelli:**

A site that once linked coeds on a college campus now links the world.

**Jason:**

And the world will never be the same.

### It's Been Said

*"When I started Facebook from my dorm room in 2004, the idea that my roommates and I talked about all the time was a world that was more open... (being) able to share the information they wanted and having access to the information they wanted is just a better world."*

Mark Zuckerberg, Facebook co-founder

## Related Threads:

- ▶ Starting Up on Facebook . . . . . . . . . . . . . . . . . . . . . 70
- ▶ Comparing Online Social Networks . . . . . . . . . . . . 36
- ▶ Facebook Special Features . . . . . . . . . . . . . . . . . . . 38
- ▶ A Knock-Off on Real Relationships? . . . . . . . . . . . 54
- ▶ Is Facebook Evil? . . . . . . . . . . . . . . . . . . . . . . . . . . . 58

**facebook** *and Your Marriage*

## Numbers Don't Lie

Average user has 130 friends on Facebook.

**What is a Facebook Friend? I've already got plenty of real friends — why do I want to find new ones on Facebook?**

### Jason & Kelli:

Time passes and we lose touch with people. Remember your best friend in elementary school? How about the kid who played shortstop on your Little League team? How did your college roommate from your freshman year do after graduation? What ever happened to so-and-so?

Facebook is a fun and easy way to reconnect with people in your past. And with hundreds of millions of people on Facebook, there's a pretty good chance you'll find them there.

But Facebook is also a way to stay better connected and informed with the people in your life right now. We stay in touch with long distance family members, friends from church, work colleagues, and the parents of our kids' friends.

### Kelli:

Jason and I have friends who live across the world from us (literally) and Facebook has helped us stay in contact with them. We share in each other's lives through sharing photos and

▶▶▶

# Facebook 411: Making Sense of Facebook

# Your BFF — Bonafide Facebook Friend

experiences regardless of the fifteen-hour time zone difference.

### Jason & Kelli:

Overall, we've found Facebook to be a great way to wipe the dust off old friendships and to add new depth to current and new friendships without much effort.

## Facebook Jargon

Facebook Friends are two Facebook users who have mutually agreed to accept each others "friendship" on Facebook which allows for a certain level of accessibility and convenient communications with one another.

## Related Threads:

- ▶ Finding Friends . . . . . . . . . . . . . . . . . . . . . . . . . . . . . .80
- ▶ Handling Friend Requests . . . . . . . . . . . . . . . . . . . . . .84
- ▶ Find-A-Friend Suggestions . . . . . . . . . . . . . . . . . . . . .86
- ▶ Creating Friend Lists . . . . . . . . . . . . . . . . . . . . . . . .112
- ▶ Friending Exes or Not? . . . . . . . . . . . . . . . . . . . . . . 164

**facebook** and Your Marriage

# Comparing Online Social Networks

Facebook 411: Making Sense of Facebook

## Did You Know?

According to Nielsen, two-thirds (67%) of global social media users visited Facebook in December 2009.

### How is Facebook different from other online social communities like MySpace and YouTube?

**Jason & Kelli:**

Facebook is the most popular, easy-to-use social network on the planet!

**Jason:**

And the others aren't.

**Jason & Kelli:**

Online social networks have been around awhile. MySpace started out catering to teenagers and giving them their own private (but publicly viewed) space. Flickr unites both sides of photo-sharing, those who take photos and those who appreciate them. YouTube links those who upload videos with those who want to view videos. And the list goes on.

Up to this point, most every online community has focused around a common interest, a shared hobby, or a particular age group.

Facebook seems to have found a way to transcend the norm for online social networks. Rather than

▶▶▶

**facebook**
and Your Marriage

36

building a network of strangers around a common interest, Facebook built a platform for people to connect with their friends and people they want to know better.

**Kelli:**

This social network centers your online community around you and those you want to have a relationship with.

## Related Threads:

- ▶ Facebook in a Nutshell........................30
- ▶ Creating Friend Lists ........................112
- ▶ Fad or Fixture?...............................56
- ▶ Starting a (Facebook) Family (Group)........136
- ▶ Finding Friends .............................80

# Facebook Special Features

Facebook 411: Making Sense of Facebook

## Our Book Club Picks

*The Missing Manual* gives you a very objective and entertaining look at everything this fascinating Facebook phenomenon has to offer.

### What all do you get when you sign up with Facebook?

### Jason & Kelli:

Every subscriber gets their own little piece of real estate within the password protected world of Facebook.

Facebook supplies you with a Wall, a Profile Page, a Home Page, an Inbox for sending private messages to other FB Friends, an Album to post and keep photos, access to tools and games to make your time on Facebook more enjoyable, and much, much more.

In addition, Facebook has set up a number of ways to help you easily find people you already know and who you would want as FB Friends. You are in total control of who you become FB Friends with.

If having your own Profile Page is not enough, you can set up or join Groups, create or become a fan of Pages, and advertise for anything you want.

Signing up for Facebook is free. No annual fees, no upgrade charges, and no monthly dues.

**facebook** and Your Marriage

Facebook 411: Making Sense of Facebook

Facebook Special Features

**Jason:**

It's a pretty amazing deal for what you get.

**Kelli:**

And you can Deactivate or Delete your account at anytime for any reason.

## Related Threads:

- ▶ The Wall . . . . . . . . . . . . . . . . . . . . . . . . . . . . . . . . . . . 50
- ▶ Facebook Email . . . . . . . . . . . . . . . . . . . . . . . . . . . . . .94
- ▶ Joining Groups & Pages . . . . . . . . . . . . . . . . . . . . . 102
- ▶ The Profile Page . . . . . . . . . . . . . . . . . . . . . . . . . . . .42
- ▶ Closing Facebook Account . . . . . . . . . . . . . . . . . . 200

**facebook**
and Your Marriage

# Can a Guy Get Some Privacy?

**Facebook 411: Making Sense of Facebook**

## Did You Know?

In a recent study, a security firm was able to access "89 percent of the users' full dates of birth, all of their e-mail addresses, where they went to school, and more."

## Facebook Jargon

Privacy Settings are a range of restrictions and protections a Facebook user can customize for their account ranging from who can view information, updates, pictures and more.

**I am really concerned about protecting my identity. What kind of privacy do I have with the information I post?**

### Jason & Kelli:

Facebook users have quite a bit of control on how much information they want to reveal and who can view it. If you want to make all your information available to everyone, you can. If you want to put your Facebook account into total lockdown, you can.

You can choose from a number of Privacy Settings, and even determine different Privacy Settings for different people or groups of FB Friends you've created.

You can choose who sees what as they're browsing around your Profile Page. You can choose what others can see when they search for you on Facebook or an outside search engine. And you can also choose what information people receive in their News Feeds.

There's also Privacy Settings related to Applications on Facebook (usually created and run by third parties).

Ultimately, it's up to you to decide how much information people can view and access.

**facebook**
*and Your Marriage*

**Jason:**

Because it can be a little overwhelming activating the Privacy Settings the way you want them, check out the step-by-step instructions at **FacebookAndYourMarriage.com.**

**It's Been Said**

*"Ten years ago, getting access to this sort of detail would... (take) a con-artist or an identity thief several weeks...many social networkers are handing over their life story on a plate."*

Sophos, a security firm

## Related Threads:

- Creating Friend Lists . . . . . . . . . . . . . . . . . . . . . . . . .112
- Removing Bad Photos . . . . . . . . . . . . . . . . . . . . . . . 188
- Something Seems Phishy . . . . . . . . . . . . . . . . . . . 194
- Hiding, Removing & Blocking People . . . . . . . . . .191
- Is Message Legit or a Scam? . . . . . . . . . . . . . . . . . 196

# The Profile Page

## Facebook 411: Making Sense of Facebook

### Facebook Jargon

The Profile Page is the only page on Facebook that is all about YOU! It contains a picture, Wall, your Contact Information, your Photo Album, a brief list of your FB Friends, and tabs to help others find more information about you.

### What is the Profile Page?

**Jason & Kelli:**

The Profile Page is the only page on Facebook that is all about YOU!

This page has your picture, your Wall, your Contact Information, your Photo Album, a brief list of your FB Friends, and tabs to help others find more information about you.

**Jason:**

But only the info you want them to see!

**Jason & Kelli:**

While the Profile Page is about you, it's not completely yours. You can't make it look the way you want it to. So, if you're used to customizing backgrounds, changing colors, and manipulating the layout of a personal page on some of the other online communities, you're going to be sorely disappointed with the lack of customization on Facebook.

**facebook** and Your Marriage

**Facebook 411: Making Sense of Facebook**

## The Profile Page

In fact, customizing your Profile Page is limited to adding a few bells and whistles through Facebook Applications like Flair, Games, Gifts, and Prizes.

**Kelli:**

But look at it this way — the time you would spend on "remodeling" your space can be spent on building relationship with your FB Friends.

## Related Threads:

- ▶ All the Fun Stuff...Applications . . . . . . . . . . . . . . . 100
- ▶ Your Profile Picture . . . . . . . . . . . . . . . . . . . . . . . . 74
- ▶ Info About Me . . . . . . . . . . . . . . . . . . . . . . . . . . . . 78
- ▶ Starting Up on Facebook . . . . . . . . . . . . . . . . . . . 70
- ▶ A Note About Notes . . . . . . . . . . . . . . . . . . . . . . . 98

**facebook** and Your Marriage

# Home Sweet Home (Page)

Facebook 411: Making Sense of Facebook

## Numbers Don't Lie

Average user clicks the Like button on 9 pieces of content each month.

**Hi! What is the Home Page all about?**

**Jason & Kelli:**

While the Profile Page is all about you, the Home Page is all about your FB Friends!

Everything your FB Friends write, upload, post, or are tagged on shows up on the Home Page. There are two primary viewing options in the News Feed (Top News and Most Recent) which display your FB Friends' posts in different ways.

The Top News displays the most relevant updates from selected FB Friends. Why do we say "selected"? Somehow and someway, Facebook determines what the most interesting postings are from your FB Friends and lists them out in the News Feed. Their method of determining what is and is not most important is as much a mystery as KFC's "secret" original recipe or how Cheez Whiz gets cheese into an aerosol bottle.

Facebook says there are a few factors including *"how many friends are commenting on a certain piece of content, who posted the content, and what type of content it is (e.g. photo, video, or status update)."*

**facebook** *and Your Marriage*

44

Facebook 411: Making Sense of Facebook

Home Sweet Home (Page)

**Jason:**

The Top News acts as a blender of certain FB Friends' past activities and recent updates.

**Jason & Kelli:**

The Most Recent view displays the most current updates made by your FB Friends and their latest Facebook activities (Groups they've joined, Pages they've become fans of, new FB Friends, etc.) as well as their posts (whether or not they include attached photos, links, and videos).

**Jason:**

Regardless of the viewing option, if you get to the end of the page and want to read more postings from more FB Friends, click on "Older Posts" link and voila, another batch of updates appears.

**Jason & Kelli:**

As you read the postings from your FB Friends, you can react or respond to what they have written by clicking on the "Comment" hotlink or indicating that you like their posting by clicking on the "Like" hotlink.

**Facebook Jargon**

The Home Page is how a Facebook user views the updates and information about all of their FB Friends. The viewing options range from Top News, Recent News, Status Updates, Photos, and more.

The top of the page and the sidebars have an array of easy-to-use links to further navigate around Facebook.

**Kelli:**

But different from the Profile Page, no customization can be done to the Home Page. But don't worry, Facebook has been known to change its look and layout quite often.

**Related Threads:**

- ▶ Making Sense of the News Feed . . . . . . . . . . . . . . . 52
- ▶ Following the Golden Rule . . . . . . . . . . . . . . . . . . . 156
- ▶ Comments — Choose Peace Not War . . . . . . . . . . 184
- ▶ Your Own Paparazzi...Sort Of . . . . . . . . . . . . . . . . . 63
- ▶ Hiding, Removing & Blocking People . . . . . . . . . . 191

# Facebook 411: Making Sense of Facebook

## Updating Your Status

**Can you help me understand how to post stuff on Facebook?**

**Jason & Kelli:**

Residing at the top of the Profile Page and the Home Page, there's a box with a statement in it called the Publisher box. This little phrase will stare you down every time you log onto Facebook.

**Kelli:**

You can answer it directly, indirectly, hypothetically, metaphorically, or ignore it all together. But this is where you post "stuff" on Facebook.

**Jason & Kelli:**

Type whatever you want into the Publisher box, click the Share button, your updated status shows up on your Wall, and all your FB Friends will be exposed to your ramblings when they view their own Home Page.

They can just read it and move on, respond to it by leaving a Comment, or let you know that they Like what you have posted.

### Numbers Don't Lie

More than 60 million status updates are posted each day.

facebook
and Your Marriage

47

## Did You Know?

More than 5 billion pieces of content (web links, news stories, blog posts, notes, photo albums, etc.) shared each week.

**Jason:**

If you want to share more than just words, the little icons below the Publisher box allow you to add a Photo, Video, Link, Event, or something else (e.g. FB Flair, FB Gifts, etc.) to your update.

This allows you to share blog articles you read, websites you like, or pictures you want to share with all of your FB Friends.

**Kelli:**

It's really easy to add them too. When you click on the little icons, a pop-up box appears and leads you through what you need to do to add the picture or URL. Facebook makes it easy for non-techy people like me to do techy things.

**Jason:**

But be aware, if you attach something to your update, depending on which Home Page viewing option your FB Friends prefer, they may not see it right away (or at all). For instance, if you attach a photo, your FB Friends may have to go to their Photos page to see the picture, which may mean that they miss it altogether.

# Facebook 411: Making Sense of Facebook

## Updating Your Status

**Jason & Kelli:**

You also have the option of determining who can see your update. Check out our website **FacebookAndYourMarriage.com** for the step-by-step instructions to "post stuff" on Facebook.

### Related Threads:

- ▶ Posting & Commenting Etiquette . . . . . . . . . . . . . . 92
- ▶ The Right Amount of Updates . . . . . . . . . . . . . . . . 88
- ▶ Following the Golden Rule . . . . . . . . . . . . . . . . . . 156
- ▶ Your Own Paparazzi...Sort Of . . . . . . . . . . . . . . . . 163
- ▶ Handling Serial Facebookers . . . . . . . . . . . . . . . . .121

### Facebook Jargon

The Publisher box is where a Facebook user types into a box located on the Profile Page and Home Page to post an update, share a Picture, a Link, a Video, an Event and more.

**facebook**
*and Your Marriage*

# The Wall

**Facebook 411: Making Sense of Facebook**

## Facebook Jargon

Facebook describes the Wall as "the center of your profile" as it is the opening page for a Facebook user's Profile Page and keeps a record of that users Facebook activity including past and current postings, lists of new FB Friends, Pages and Groups that have been joined and more. It is also where FB Friends can leave messages.

**I've heard people refer to "the wall," but I don't see anything that looks like a wall. What is it?**

### Jason & Kelli:

Every subscriber has a public message board called a Wall. It is found on the opening screen of the Profile Page. It is so important that Facebook describes it as *"the center of your profile."*

### Jason:

The tab at the top of the Profile Page should read "Wall" (and be highlighted differently than the other tabs). The large center column is the Wall.

### Jason & Kelli:

You can post things to the Wall, your FB Friends can write on it and they can view it too. The Wall is the catch basin for all your Facebook activities, including your last several updates (as well as Comments by your FB Friends on your postings), people you've recently become FB Friends with, and any Links, Pictures, Videos, or Notes you've posted publicly.

▶▶▶

**facebook**
*and Your Marriage*

50

**Facebook 411: Making Sense of Facebook**

# The Wall

**Kelli:**

If there's something on your Wall that you don't want on there, you can remove it.

**Jason:**

You can also set it up so certain FB Friends can see only what you want them to see on the Wall.

## Related Threads:

- Can a Guy Get Some Privacy? ................40
- Relationship Status..........................76
- Your Profile Picture........................74
- A Note About Notes.........................98
- Posting & Commenting Etiquette .............92

**facebook** *and Your Marriage*

# Making Sense of the News Feed

**Facebook 411: Making Sense of Facebook**

## Facebook Jargon

The News Feed is the default view for a Facebook users Home Page, with two primary views: Top News and Recent News.

**What's the difference between Top News and Most Recent on the News Feed?**

### Jason & Kelli:

If you have an insatiable appetite for knowing "the latest" rather than "the greatest" about people, then the Most Recent News Feed may be what you want to view on your Home Page.

### Jason:

The Most Recent News Feed does not have a super secret, specially designed filter like the Top News News Feed does.

### Jason & Kelli:

Top News shows all the latest Facebook activities of your FB Friends, including anything they've posted (Status Update, Photos, Videos, Links, etc.) or anything they've been tagged in (Video, Photo, Notes, etc.) or anything they've joined (Groups, Pages) or new people they've become FB Friends with.

▶▶▶

**facebook**
*and Your Marriage*

**Kelli:**

There is also a way to edit who is and is not included in the feeds and how many FB Friends' postings can be seen. Go to **FacebookAndYourMarriage.com** for more info on the Home Page viewing options.

## Related Threads:

- Can a Guy Get Some Privacy? . . . . . . . . . . . . . . . . . 40
- What the @ Is This? . . . . . . . . . . . . . . . . . . . . . . . 124
- Sharing Pictures . . . . . . . . . . . . . . . . . . . . . . . . . .116
- Reducing Activities Reporting . . . . . . . . . . . . . . . 198
- Quiz & Game Notifications . . . . . . . . . . . . . . . . . 128

# A Knock-Off on Real Relationships

**Facebook 411: Making Sense of Facebook**

## It's Been Said

"People can connect better with the people around them, understand more of what's going on with the people around them, and understand more in general."

Mark Zuckerberg, Facebook co-founder

---

**As a society, I think we spend too much time looking at screens and not enough time talking to real people. Doesn't Facebook just rob us of our real-life relationships?**

**Jason & Kelli:**

Computers are and always will be a part of our lives. What we do with them and how much time is consumed by them is a matter of setting personal boundaries.

We have found Facebook to be a great way to go deeper with a lot more friends and family we wouldn't have the time or energy to connect with. Whether our FB Friends live down the block, around the world, or somewhere in between, regularly sharing our lives with one another online (viewing and sharing pictures and reading updates) can really enhance our real-life experiences with them.

**Jason:**

My cousin moved from Seattle to Tennessee a few years ago. While he's been away, we've stayed connected through Facebook. When I saw him at a recent family gathering, we were able to jump past the small talk and predictable pleasantries and engage on what has been going on in

▶▶▶

**facebook** and Your Marriage

each other's lives. It made the live, face-to-face experience much more dynamic and interesting.

### Kelli:

I have found that Facebook has helped me stay in better touch with what is going on with our neighbors and local friends. When I run into a FB Friend at the grocery store or coffee shop or a soccer practice, I've found that my live conversation with them is less superficial and much more personal.

### Jason & Kelli:

But you do bring up a valid concern. It is important for us to make sure there is balance between fostering our relationships online and in real life.

## Related Threads:

- ▶ Avoiding FB Addiction...................148
- ▶ Go on Facebook Dates...................214
- ▶ The "About Us" Date ...................334
- ▶ Setting Up Boundaries..................319
- ▶ Living Inbounds........................344

# Fad or Fixture?

Facebook 411: Making Sense of Facebook

## Numbers Don't Lie

More than 400 million active users are on Facebook.

**Isn't Facebook just another online craze that will be hot for a while and then fade away?**

### Jason & Kelli:

If Facebook were a country, it would be one of the largest nations in the world. With hundreds of millions of members and surging trends in every demographic, Facebook isn't going away tomorrow.

### Jason:

Will Facebook be around in two years, five years, or ten years from now? Nobody knows.

### Jason & Kelli:

Technology will change. Will Facebook endure long-term through the changing technological advancements and fickle consumer wants like Amazon or Google? Or will Facebook fizzle out and be forgotten in the cyberspace black hole of countless trendy but short-lived websites?

In our opinion, Facebook has done something that most every other online community has not. It has mainstreamed the experience of being

▶▶▶

facebook
and Your Marriage

# Facebook 411: Making Sense of Facebook

## Fad or Fixture?

part of an online social network across all age, geographic, and ethnic demographics.

### Kelli:

So, regardless of what happens to Facebook in the future, many of us have gotten a taste of being part of an online social community and we really, really like it!

### Did You Know?

Facebook is growing by half a million new users every day.

## Related Threads:

- ▶ Comparing Online Social Networks . . . . . . . . . . . . . 36
- ▶ Facebook's Conception, Birth & First Steps . . . . . . 32
- ▶ A Knock-Off on Real Relationships . . . . . . . . . . . . . 54
- ▶ Tweeting Facebook, Facebooking Twitter . . . . . . 132
- ▶ Linking Your Phone & Facebook . . . . . . . . . . . . . . 130

## facebook
### and Your Marriage

Is Facebook Evil?  Facebook 411: Making Sense of Facebook

**Did You Know?**

Love Without Boundaries raised almost $150,000 through Causes allowing the organization to provide medical care to orphans in China.

**I have a friend who thinks that Facebook is the "devil's tool." Her sister's husband left his marriage for another woman he found on Facebook. My friend thinks the bad far outweighs any good that can come from Facebook. How would you respond to her?**

**Jason & Kelli:**

Facebook isn't for everybody.

And yes, bad things have happened to marriages and families from people meeting or reconnecting on Facebook. But is that Facebook's fault, or the fault of the people who chose to turn their back on their wedding vows and head straight into an affair?

But there is a lot of good that has resulted from Facebook. Non-profits and churches are raising awareness of their great causes through Facebook. Vital information gets passed throughout Facebook at a faster clip than the newspapers or television news could ever get the information out. Long lost family members are reuniting, childhood friendships are being given a second life, and people are finding help for their problems and issues.

▶▶▶

**facebook**
and Your Marriage

58

Facebook 411: Making Sense of Facebook Is Facebook Evil?

**Jason:**

So who gets the credit for all the good stuff happening on Facebook? The devil? Facebook?

**Kelli:**

I say it's the people who use Facebook as a vehicle for good, helpful, and honorable purposes.

**Jason & Kelli:**

It grieves our hearts when we hear stories or read news articles about how a marriage broke up. But that's like blaming an SUV for an accident or a gun for a shooting when it is really user error. What happens on Facebook is the full responsibility of the adults who made the decision to start the Facebook account in the first place.

### Did You Know?

The Aflac Cancer Center and Blood Disorders Service of Children's Healthcare of Atlanta has raised over one-million dollars by being listed as a Facebook Cause.

## Related Threads:

- ▸ Let Facebook Know You're Married . . . . . . . . . . . 150
- ▸ The R.D.A. for Facebook . . . . . . . . . . . . . . . . . . 142
- ▸ Dealing with Flirts . . . . . . . . . . . . . . . . . . . . . . . 126
- ▸ Setting Up Boundaries . . . . . . . . . . . . . . . . . . . 319
- ▸ Creating Your Own Boundaries . . . . . . . . . . . . . 341

facebook
and Your Marriage

# Should Married Facebookers Beware?

*Facebook 411: Making Sense of Facebook*

**Did You Know?**

What every Facebooking couple should do:

Create boundaries

Set Relationship Status to "Married"

Update each other on FB Friends

Share username and password

Make spouse a post topic weekly

---

**I'm reading in the news about horror stories of spouses leaving their marriage for a lost love they've rediscovered on Facebook. Is it a mistake to be married and on Facebook?**

**Jason & Kelli:**

We've read the stories too. A wife leaves her husband for a man she met on Facebook. A husband gets caught up in an emotional affair. A husband issues the "first Facebook divorce notice" to his wife when she reads his update, "Neil Brady has ended his marriage to Emma Brady."

It is true that some people have made some really bad decisions and poor choices during their Facebook experience.

**Kelli:**

And some have made some really poor choices as a result of what they did through Facebook.

**Jason & Kelli:**

While the bulk of Facebookers aren't losing their marriages or having emotional affairs on Facebook, situations will arise that all couples need to be prepared for: Friend Requests by old boyfriends/girlfriends, Chats that turn weird,

▶▶▶

**facebook**
*and Your Marriage*

60

# Facebook 411: Making Sense of Facebook

# Should Married Facebookers Beware?

messages in the FB Inbox from an opposite sex friend.

With agreed upon boundaries, open and honest dialogue, and frequent communication, couples can avoid these kinds of scenarios.

### Jason:

And even if their marriage is heading down the pathway of being a potential sensationalized infidelity news story, couples can overcome most any form of betrayal.

### Jason & Kelli:

This is the main reason we wrote *Facebook and Your Marriage*! Sections 2 and 3 address more Facebook basics.

**Section 4** helps you set up some simple safeguards for your marriage, your spouse, and yourself.

**Section 5** prepares you to expect the unexpected and Facebook surprises.

**Section 6** feeds you all kinds of ideas to spice up your marriage using Facebook.

**Section 7** provides guidance and input to spouses who feel like Facebook is becoming a threat to their marriage.

## Making a Difference

**Smart Marriages**
The Coalition for Marriage, Family, and Couples Education

Smart Marriages is dedicated to making Marriage and Relationship Education widely available — to getting the information couples need out of the research labs and to the public through user-friendly, affordable, marriage and relationship education programs and resources.

**facebook** and Your Marriage

**Section 8** is directed toward those spouses who are intentionally or unintentionally allowing their Facebook experience to jeopardize their marriage.

**Section 9** provides couples with the insights and skills to talk offline about online issues. Finally,

**Section 10** points readers to more resources and help for their Facebook experience and their marriage relationship.

## Related Threads:

- K.I.S.S. — Simple Ways to Safeguard Your Marriage, Your Spouse, and Yourself . . . . . . 140
- Surprise! How to Expect the Unexpected and Not Sweat It . . . . . . . . . . . . . . . . . . . . . . . . . . . 172
- Let's Get It On! Have a Facebook Affair... With Your Spouse! . . . . . . . . . . . . . . . . . . . . . . . . . 202
- SOS! My Marriage Is Suffering Because of Facebook! . . . . . . . . . . . . . . . . . . . . . . . 230
- Seriously? Let's Think This Through a Bit More . . 278
- TMI! Talking with Your Mate Offline About Online Issues . . . . . . . . . . . . . . . . . . . . . . . . . 312
- Back of The Book Stuff . . . . . . . . . . . . . . . . . . . . . . 352

# Facebook 411: Making Sense of Facebook

# Your Own Paparazzi...Sort Of

**C'mon! I'm not that interesting of a person. Do people really care what I'm thinking or doing?**

**Jason:**

More than you know!

**Jason & Kelli:**

Facebook was designed to help people stay connected with one another. When people accept you as a FB Friend, that is their way of saying "I care!" If you don't know what to write for your posting, read what others are writing to discover what kind of updates you like and what kind you don't like.

When you finally dare to write something, be prepared for a variety of different responses from your FB Friends. In fact, we've found five types of common responders on Facebook.

1. **The Over Doer**

    The Over Doer seems to be on Facebook 24/7 and responds and comments on virtually everything.

## Our Book Club Picks

*Facebook Me!* by Dave Awl helps you find out what you can do on Facebook, and what it can do for you. Reconnect with old friends and make new ones, let your friends know what you're up to, send greetings, share photos or video, or just goof around with applications.

**facebook**
*and Your Marriage*

**Did You Know?**

Six of the 12 most annoying Facebookers (according to CNN.com) include: the Self-Promoter, the Friend-Padder, the TMIer, the Bad Grammarian, the Chronic Inviter, and the Let-Me-Tell-You-Every-Detail-of-My-Day Bore.

2. **The Newby**

   The Newby is new to Facebook and hasn't mastered the difference between a Wall, a FB Email, or a Comment on an update. The Newby will inadvertently hijack a post and instead of referencing the topic in the post, they'll ask you about how you're doing or for your mom's broccoli salad recipe.

3. **The Self-Appointed Killjoy**

   The Self-Appointed Killjoy takes the fun and free flowing exchange of posts and comments and quickly turn the tone and intensity in another direction.

4. **The Voyeur**

   The Voyeur will never types a Comment or Wall Post. They read your updates and move on.

5. **The Happy Facebooker**

   The Happy Facebooker gives a healthy dose of Comments or chooses the Like button to show they're there, reading and appreciating you without being involved in every post.

So find out how many people really care and begin posting something.

**Jason:**

You'll be amazed at the "FB love" you'll receive, and even more so, surprised from who you get it.

**Kelli:**

Just wait until your birthday. You'll get ten times as many well-wishes from people on Facebook than you do from people in real life.

## Related Threads:

- ▶ Updating Your Status . . . . . . . . . . . . . . . . . . . . . . . . . 47
- ▶ The Right Amount of Updates . . . . . . . . . . . . . . . . 88
- ▶ When Private Stuff Goes Public . . . . . . . . . . . . . . . 186
- ▶ Comments — Choose Peace Not War . . . . . . . . . 184
- ▶ Posting & Commenting Etiquette . . . . . . . . . . . . . 92

*Hundreds of millions of people have taken the plunge and joined Facebook. When first getting started, they all wrestled with many of the issues dealt with in this series of threads. Find beneficial answers to questions you may not even know you have (yet).*

## Section 2

▸ Joint or Solo Account?................................68
▸ Starting Up on Facebook.............................70
▸ Maiden or Married Name?...........................72
▸ Your Profile Picture..................................74
▸ Relationship Status..................................76
▸ Info About Me .......................................78
▸ Finding Friends......................................80
▸ Friend Swap with Spouse?..........................82
▸ Handling Friend Requests..........................84
▸ Find-A-Friend Suggestions.........................86
▸ The Right Amount of Updates......................88
▸ Your Friends Are Hot (Linked)!.....................90
▸ Posting & Commenting Etiquette..................92
▸ Facebook Email......................................94
▸ About the Chat Feature ............................96
▸ A Note About Notes.................................98
▸ All the Fun Stuff...Applications...................100
▸ Joining Groups & Pages............................102

# C'mon! Join the Rest of the Planet on Facebook

# Joint or Solo Account?

C'mon! Join the Rest of the Planet on Facebook

## Making a Difference

**growthtrac**

Growthtrac builds strong marriages through life-changing marriage resources offered through their website.

### Should my hubby and I set up one joint profile or two individual profiles?

### Jason & Kelli:

This isn't quite the equivalent of whether a bride should take her husband's last name, hyphenate, or keep her maiden name, but it's as close as you get on Facebook.

The vast majority of married Facebookers set up an individual account and then link their account with their spouse's account and mark themselves as "Married." We have seen a few couples create a joint Facebook account. Some have used both first names or they use the family's last name.

It's up to you to figure out the pros and cons of setting up a joint Facebook account and see what makes the most sense.

A joint account could limit the people you connect with on Facebook because the search engine on Facebook for people to find friends is built around past schools you've graduated from, companies you've worked for, and names of people. While we're big believers in "the two become one" idea of marriage, we each have our own histories and set of relationships that involve different people. It will make it more difficult for people to find you or your spouse with a joint account.

**facebook** and Your Marriage

Also, a joint account could keep some FB Friends from freely corresponding with you because they don't know who is on the other side of the screen.

**Kelli:**

If you do set up a joint account, when updating your status or making comments on other people's posts, it is really helpful for readers if you add your name or your initials at the end of the message.

**Jason:**

BTW, according to Facebook, *"Accounts can represent one person only. Accounts representing groups, families, or couples are not allowed."* For whatever it's worth. It's up to you.

**Numbers Don't Lie**

Women make up nearly six-in-ten (57%) of the Facebook audience but males (ages 13-35) are growing as an audience faster than females in the same age range.

## Related Threads:

- Relationship Status..............................76
- Password Exchange ..........................146
- Finding Mutual Friends ...................... 158
- Sharing the Love Through Updates............208
- Setting Up Boundaries........................ 319

# Starting Up on Facebook

C'mon! Join the Rest of the Planet on Facebook

**Did You Know?**

Five tips to keep your time on Facebook safe.

1. Hide your year of birth
2. Change your password often
3. Keep your private info private
4. Remove friends as appropriate
5. Monitor suspicious activity

**My husband is finally going to join Facebook. It's been forever since I joined. Can you remind me of the steps he needs to take to start a profile?**

**Jason & Kelli:**

Let us be the first to bid congrats to your hubby on joining Facebook.

Have him go to www.facebook.com. There on the main page is the Sign Up form that he can start filling out.

**Kelli:**

You've probably become so accustomed to seeing it when you log in that you don't see it anymore.

**Jason & Kelli:**

Once he begins, he'll be prompted through the process of setting up his Facebook account including, adding a Profile Picture, adding personal and contact information, and finding FB Friends.

▶▶▶

**facebook**
*and Your Marriage*

**Jason:**

All he needs to get started is an email address (something other than a work email address is preferred), about 15 minutes of time, and the ability to follow prompted directions.

## Related Threads:

- ▶ Your Profile Picture............................74
- ▶ Info About Me ................................78
- ▶ Password Exchange .........................146
- ▶ Let Facebook Know You're Married...........150
- ▶ Creating Your Own Boundaries ..............341

# Maiden or Married Name?

## Our Book Club Picks

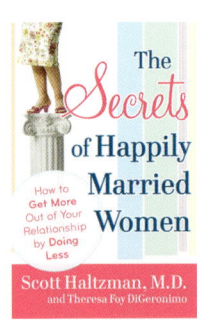

In *The Secrets of Happily Married Women*, Dr. Haltzman tells stories from real women who are happy in their relationships. They know how to get more out of their partners by doing less, by not trying so hard to make men perfect, not dragging them to couples therapy, and not expecting them to think or behave like a woman.

**What do you think? For my Profile name, should I use my maiden name or my married name or both?**

### Jason & Kelli:

People only search names they know, and for a married woman that creates a challenge since most people from the past know her by her maiden name, not her married name.

In the past, women who have changed their last name have had to type their maiden name into the middle name box in order for people they've known from their pre-married days to search and find them.

Facebook has since liberated the middle names of millions of women by creating a feature to insert maiden names without having to misuse the middle name box. This allows for easier searches and more accurate Friend Requests.

### Jason:

And the true essence of the middle name box to be reserved for its intended use (since some of us — including me — use our middle name as our common name).

**facebook** and Your Marriage

# C'mon! Join the Rest of the Planet on Facebook

# Maiden or Married Name?

**Kelli:**

So ladies, you can confidently go by both your married and maiden names and not worry if people who've known you as either name will be able to find you on Facebook. If you still need help, go to **FacebookAndYourMarriage.com** for step-by-step instructions on setting your full name up correctly.

### Related Threads:

- Finding Friends . . . . . . . . . . . . . . . . . . . . . . . . . . . . . . 80
- Linking Your Phone & Facebook . . . . . . . . . . . . . . 130
- Setting Up Boundaries . . . . . . . . . . . . . . . . . . . . . . . 319
- Let Facebook Know You're Married . . . . . . . . . . . 150
- Friending Exes . . . . . . . . . . . . . . . . . . . . . . . . . . . . . 164

### Transform Your Relationship

**Couple Checkup**
PREPARE ENRICH

The Couple Checkup is designed to help couples build a more satisfying and intimate relationship. This online relationship inventory is designed to activate dialogue, discovery, and increase the overall quality of your relationship through highlighting your strengths as a couple.

## facebook
### and Your Marriage

# Your Profile Picture

C'mon! Join the Rest of the Planet on Facebook

## Facebook Jargon

The Profile Picture is the picture Facebook users choose to post on their Profile Page and it becomes the primary image FB Friends see and associate with the user's updates, postings, and comments. The Profile Picture can be changed at any time.

### How do I load a picture onto my Profile?

**Jason & Kelli:**

Before you can load a picture onto Facebook, you must have a digital file on your computer or phone to upload. To load up a picture, click on the space where your Profile Picture is to appear and follow the prompts.

The only photos that aren't allowed are copyrighted pictures (unless you own the copyright). Other than that, you can load fun, casual pictures or formal professional photos. You can have a Profile Picture with you and your spouse, your kids, or your grandkids in the picture. You can switch out your Profile Picture and change it on a regular basis. Keeping the Profile Picture fresh and current is not hard to do.

**Jason:**

Just make sure YOU are IN the Profile Picture. This may be my own personal gripe, but it is really frustrating to get a Friend Request from someone whose name you kind of recognize but the Profile Picture is of a little baby or an animal.

**facebook** and Your Marriage

# Your Profile Picture

**Kelli:**

I think it's cute.

**Jason:**

Great! Put the picture in the FB Album and write endless amounts of comments about how adorable the baby is or how great the dog is. Just don't make it your Profile Picture.

**Kelli:**

It is fun to swap out your Profile Picture a bit though. An old wedding photo or high school yearbook pictures can be fun to see from time-to-time. Plus for those who knew you a lifetime ago, its like, "Oh, that's who you were!" ☺

## Related Threads:

- ▶ The Profile Page . . . . . . . . . . . . . . . . . . . . . . . . . . . . . 42
- ▶ Sharing Pictures . . . . . . . . . . . . . . . . . . . . . . . . . . . . .116
- ▶ Removing Bad Photos . . . . . . . . . . . . . . . . . . . . . . . 188
- ▶ Show `Em More Love . . . . . . . . . . . . . . . . . . . . . . . . 212
- ▶ Maiden or Married Name? . . . . . . . . . . . . . . . . . . . . 72

**facebook** and Your Marriage

# Relationship Status

### Facebook Jargon

Relationship Status is a Facebook user's way to announce their marital status to others on Facebook.

**Do y'all think I should fill out my relationship status? My wife thinks I should but I don't think it really matters.**

### Jason & Kelli:

With Facebook, you don't have to do anything you don't want to do.

But, while you're not required to state your Relationship Status, we strongly encourage you to mark your Relationship Status as "Married."

### Jason:

Your Relationship Status acts like a wedding ring on Facebook. It tells others you're married and can help you (and others) avoid situations or comments that leave both parties feeling uncomfortable and embarrassed.

### Kelli:

I overheard two college-aged girls talking about guys they've been dating. One asked the other, "Are you Facebook serious?" Apparently changing one's Relationship Status on Facebook is a sign of the seriousness in a dating relationship.

**Jason:**

If dating couples see it as a big deal, married couples should too.

**Jason & Kelli:**

As your list of FB Friends grows, there's a pretty good chance that some of them won't know much about your life, including if you're married or not. Don't leave it a mystery for others to discover by accident; mark your Relationship Status as "Married" and leave it that way unless something drastically changes…legally.

## Related Threads:

- Joint or Solo Account?...........................68
- Dealing With Flirts ............................ 126
- Let Facebook Know You're Married............ 150
- Changing My Status to "It's Complicated"......288
- Spouse Changes "Married" to "It's Complicated" 264

# Info About Me

C'mon! Join the Rest of the Planet on Facebook

## Did You Know?

If you use your birthdate, maiden name or kids' names for passwords and personal identification numbers, broadcasting that information could help identity theft criminals pose as you when they log on to various web sites.

### How much information should I share in the About Me profile?

**Jason & Kelli:**

Only post as much information as you feel comfortable with.

Keep in mind that current and future FB Friends will often view this section, as it's a way for them to get to know you better. It is also a way for advertisers to target you with certain ads.

Be careful of how much personal information you put here. Avoid listing your physical address, any private numbers, email addresses or contact information, or the year on your birth date. These bits of info can go a long way for a scammer, a spammer, or a thief to use.

Also, watch the words and the attitude with your responses to the topics. Keep the reader in mind when you're filling it out.

**Jason:**

Sometimes a person's attempt to be funny on topics like religion or politics can be offensive. People tend to be more emboldened when they type. Try speaking your responses out loud, and think about how they will land with someone you

▶▶▶

**facebook**
*and Your Marriage*

know who has a different opinion. Would you say these words to someone's face? What would be their natural reaction?

**Kelli:**

Even though this is an online community, you likely have or have had a real-time relationship with many of your FB Friends. Respect in the real world is the same respect we need to show online.

**Jason & Kelli:**

If you do end up leaving a box blank, the topic doesn't show up blank. It won't show up at all.

## Related Threads:

- Can a Guy Get Some Privacy? . . . . . . . . . . . . . . . . . 40
- Following the Golden Rule . . . . . . . . . . . . . . . . . . 156
- Something Seems Phishy . . . . . . . . . . . . . . . . . . . 194
- International Friend Requests . . . . . . . . . . . . . . . 182
- Is Message Legit or a Scam? . . . . . . . . . . . . . . . . . 196

# Finding Friends

### C'mon! Join the Rest of the Planet on Facebook

## Transform Your Relationship

Celebrate Your Marriage is a marriage conference providing couples with first-rate destinations along with world-class entertainment and Biblical teaching. Hosted by Jay and Laura Laffoon, couples get time to connect and enjoy time together.

## How do I find friends and family?

### Jason & Kelli:

Facebook has got to have one of the easiest systems to quickly and simply find friends and family. And once you become FB Friends with people, Facebook begins looking for others who share a common FB Friend, Page or Group and makes suggestions to you.

But you have to get started. So click on Friends and you'll find several ways to find acquaintances, friends, co-workers, family, classmates, and anyone else you have any sort of association with.

Or you can type random names into the Search box.

Once you find some FB Friends, scroll through their list of Friends to find others you can invite to be your FB Friends (as long as you know them).

### Kelli:

When I send Friend Requests to people from my pre-married life, I send a message along with the request that references where I know them from along with my maiden name. That helps them decide if they want to accept it or not.

▶▶▶

**facebook** and Your Marriage

80

**Jason:**

You'll find some more friend-finding help at **FacebookAndYourMarriage.com**.

## Related Threads:

- ▶ Your BFF — Bonafide Facebook Friend . . . . . . . . . 34
- ▶ Handling Friend Requests . . . . . . . . . . . . . . . . . . . . . 84
- ▶ Declining Friend Requests with Dignity . . . . . . . . . 118
- ▶ Friend Requests from Old Flames . . . . . . . . . . . . . 179
- ▶ Finding Help . . . . . . . . . . . . . . . . . . . . . . . . . . . . . . . . 349

# Friend Swap With Spouse?

C'mon! Join the Rest of the Planet on Facebook

## Did You Know?

In a recent study, a security firm found that 41%-46% of people "blindly accepted" friend requests from two fake Facebook users.

### Should I become friends with everyone my husband is friends with?

**Jason & Kelli:**

Unless you and your husband are both friends or acquaintances with someone, you shouldn't feel compelled to become FB Friends with all the same people. Past school or work friendships, current co-workers and general friendships are going to be different for both of you.

**Jason:**

As of this writing, I have over 920 FB Friends and Kelli has 584 FB Friends. We have about 240 FB Friends in common.

**Jason & Kelli:**

It is important that you and your husband know who each of you are sending Friend Requests to and whose Friend Requests you're accepting.

**facebook** and Your Marriage

**Kelli:**

And if for any reason, either of you is uncomfortable with the FB Friend, then they've got to go (the FB Friend that is ☺).

## Related Threads:

- ▶ Friending Exes...or Nor?. . . . . . . . . . . . . . . . . . . . . . 164
- ▶ Friending an Ex-Spouse. . . . . . . . . . . . . . . . . . . . . . 167
- ▶ Hiding, Removing & Blocking People . . . . . . . . . . .191
- ▶ Finding Mutual Friends . . . . . . . . . . . . . . . . . . . . . 158
- ▶ Setting Boundaries. . . . . . . . . . . . . . . . . . . . . . . . . 319

# Handling Friend Requests

C'mon! Join the Rest of the Planet on Facebook

## Numbers Don't Lie

The average Facebook user sends 8 friend requests per month.

**I am getting a lot of requests to become FB Friends with people. It's a little overwhelming. Can you help me out here?**

### Jason & Kelli:

Facebook is a booster shot for the ego.

### Kelli:

You can kind of have your Sally Fields moment when a Friend Request happens: *"You like me. You really like me."*

### Jason:

Or you have your "Oh crap!" moment. *"I don't really enjoy you in real life and I really don't want to spend more time with you on Facebook."*

### Jason & Kelli:

Even though Facebook is an online community, becoming FB Friends with people is a form of bonding. Anytime you're considering a Friend Request (either accepting one or sending one), ask yourself a couple of questions.

*"Am I really interested in what this person has to say and getting updated on their life?"*

▶▶▶

## facebook
### and Your Marriage

# Handling Friend Requests

*"Am I comfortable with this person reading what I have to say and knowing what is going on in my life?"*

If the answer is "Yes," you have a new FB Friend. If either answer is "No," then you have a choice to make. Do you refuse their Friend Request, or do you accept the Friend Request and then Hide their updates from view?

## Facebook Jargon

Facebook users are notified of Friend Requests as they occur. When a Facebook user decides they want to connect with another user on Facebook, they send a Friend Request. The receiver then has the option to "accept" or "ignore" the Friend Request.

## Related Threads:

- ▶ Find-A-Friend Suggestions .................... 86
- ▶ Handling Serial Facebookers ................. 121
- ▶ Declining Friend Requests with Dignity ......... 118
- ▶ Creating Your Own Boundaries .............. 341
- ▶ Hiding, Removing & Blocking People .......... 191

# Find-A-Friend Suggestions

## Facebook Jargon

Friend Suggestions occur due to Facebook's automated system that cross references the FB Friends of a user and searches for common links with other users. The recommendations may or may not be someone the user has ever known or associated with.

**The friend suggestions list a lot of people I don't really know and recommends I become a fan of things I don't really care about. How do I remove the unwanted recommendations off the list?**

### Jason & Kelli:

While the Suggestions feature is helpful at times, it can be a little obnoxious because Facebook is making a calculated guess a lot of the time.

Facebook has an automated system that cross references the FB Friends of your FB Friends and tries to determine if there is some sort of link (by number of mutual friends) even when there may be none. A similar approach is taken with Pages and Groups, although it seems that when one of your FB Friends becomes a fan of a Page or joins a Group, you are given a recommendation to follow their actions.

To reject the recommendations, simply place the cursor on the X, click it, and the suggestion will disappear.

### Kelli:

Keep in mind that Facebook takes the philosophy that *"a 'no' today doesn't mean 'no' tomorrow."* You will likely see the same Friend, Page, and Group suggestions again some time in the future.

▶▶▶

facebook
and Your Marriage

**Jason:**

So don't worry if you have a happy trigger finger deleting the recommendations. They'll be back at a later date.

**Jason & Kelli:**

One way to reduce the annoyance you're feeling is to let the recommendations accumulate and view them once a week rather than every time the Suggestions feature displays a suggested FB Friend, Page, or Group.

## Related Threads:

- ▶ Handling Friend Requests . . . . . . . . . . . . . . . . . . . . . . .84
- ▶ Creating Friend Lists . . . . . . . . . . . . . . . . . . . . . . . . . .112
- ▶ Joining Groups & Pages . . . . . . . . . . . . . . . . . . . . . . . 102
- ▶ Friending Exes...or Not? . . . . . . . . . . . . . . . . . . . . . . 164
- ▶ Spouse Overreacting on Friend Choices . . . . . . .284

# The Right Amount of Updates

C'mon! Join the Rest of the Planet on Facebook

## Numbers Don't Lie

More than 35 million users update their status each day.

### How many times should I update my status and what kinds of things should I write about?

**Jason & Kelli:**

There is no magic number for the amount of times someone should update their status. Some people send updates every once in awhile and others update multiple times throughout the day. A good rule of thumb is no more than five times a day. Shoot for at least one update a day, and make it more or less from there.

The question in the Publisher box can be somewhat intimidating. Do your FB Friends really want to know what's going on in between your ears?

When getting started on Facebook, it's a good idea to sit back and watch what other FB Friends are writing about. From this safe vantage point, you'll be able to view a range of updates from interesting to pointless, from intriguing to annoying, from funny to bland.

Keep in mind that most people who read your update will have little or no frame of reference about the details of your life, so be sure to give enough information for your FB Friends to understand what you're writing about without overwhelming them with details.

Be fully aware of who could possibly be reading

▶▶▶

facebook
and Your Marriage

your update (family, spouse, kids, friends, co-workers, neighbors) and think of them before you push the "Share" or "Comment" button.

### Jason:

Avoid sharing too much unwanted information (like *"I'm so constipated! Anyone got home remedies to get the pipes unstuck?"*).

### Kelli:

Eww!

Also, avoid giving people a blow-by-blow account of the day ahead...we really don't care to know the details of your daily schedule. No offense.

## Related Threads:

- ▶ Posting & Commenting Etiquette . . . . . . . . . . . . . . 92
- ▶ Sharing Pictures . . . . . . . . . . . . . . . . . . . . . . . . . . . 116
- ▶ Making Web Links Work . . . . . . . . . . . . . . . . . . . . 114
- ▶ Handling Serial Facebookers . . . . . . . . . . . . . . . . 121
- ▶ Your Friends Are Hot (Linked!) . . . . . . . . . . . . . . . 90

# Your Friends Are Hot (Linked)!

## C'mon! Join the Rest of the Planet on Facebook

### Transform Your Relationship

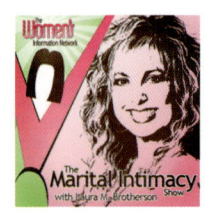

The Marital Intimacy Show is hosted by Laura M. Brotherson, intimacy expert and bestselling author. She takes on the taboo subject of sex, shining a light into the intricacies of intimacy and marriage. The Marital Intimacy Show provides straight talk about empowering women (and couples) to create the relationship of their dreams.

**I've noticed some Status Updates where a person is referenced and it links to the person's profile. How do I do that?**

**Jason & Kelli:**

Some people claim that Facebook stole this idea from Twitter, but regardless, hotlinking names within a posting is a great idea that further connects, identifies, and in some cases promotes the one being written about.

Commonly, people just reference someone's first name in their Status Update:

"Went to the coffee shop after church and ran into our old neighbors Jeremy and Leanne. My wife and I really miss them."

By hotlinking names in your Status Update, you're kind of introducing your FB Friends to other FB Friends, Groups, and/or Pages.

"Went to Starbucks after church at New Life Church Renton and ran into our old neighbors Jeremy Johnson and Leanne Burt Johnson. My wife Kelli Krafsky and I really miss them."

All you have to do is type the @ sign and begin typing a name. (There should be no space between the @ sign and the name.) A drop box will appear with your FB Friends, Groups, or Pages in it. The more you type, the more specific the list becomes, allowing you to click on your choice and voila,

▶▶▶

**facebook**
*and Your Marriage*

90

their name is hotlinked in your update.

When you press "Share", the update shows up on your Wall, their Home Page (and the Home Page of all your FB Friends), and it also appears on their Wall. This allows your hotlinked FB Friend to see the post with their name in it without having to be on Facebook at the time the comment was posted.

## Related Threads:

- ▶ Joining Groups & Pages . . . . . . . . . . . . . . . . . . . . . . 102
- ▶ Making Web Links Work . . . . . . . . . . . . . . . . . . . . .114
- ▶ The Wall . . . . . . . . . . . . . . . . . . . . . . . . . . . . . . . . . . .50
- ▶ Updating Your Status . . . . . . . . . . . . . . . . . . . . . . . . 47
- ▶ Posting & Commenting Etiquette . . . . . . . . . . . . . 92

**facebook**
and Your Marriage

# Posting & Commenting Etiquette

## C'mon! Join the Rest of the Planet on Facebook

### Numbers Don't Lie

Average user writes 25 comments on Facebook content each month.

### Is there anything I shouldn't do or say in my posts?

**Jason & Kelli:**

Be careful little hands what you type.

Be careful little hands what you type.

For the people on Facebook

Are reading what you write.

So be careful little hands what you type.

Keep in mind that a lot of different people are reading what you write (and if someone comments on it, their FB Friends who may not be your FB Friends see it too). Kids, grandparents, bosses, pastors, teachers, neighbors, and other people's spouses are all on Facebook.

Here are three no-no's when it comes to writing a post or a comment:

1. Swearing (it's immature)
2. Sex references (it's crude)
3. Calling out someone by name on a private matter (it's really tacky)

**Kelli:**

For safety's sake, avoid giving out too many details, especially when you, your spouse, or your family is out of town. And especially if your address is posted on the Info tab of your Profile Page. This is a bad combo that makes your home, your property and your family vulnerable.

## Related Threads:

- ▶ Updating Your Status . . . . . . . . . . . . . . . . . . . . . . . . . . 47
- ▶ Following the Golden Rule . . . . . . . . . . . . . . . . . . . 156
- ▶ Handling Serial Facebookers . . . . . . . . . . . . . . . . . . .121
- ▶ Sharing the Love Through Updates . . . . . . . . . . . .208
- ▶ Handling Embarrassing Comments . . . . . . . . . . . . 170

# Facebook Email

C'mon! Join the Rest of the Planet on Facebook

## Facebook Jargon

Facebook users have access to an Inbox that is attached to their account. It allows users to send emails to FB Friends and even to people without a Facebook account. While similar to regular email accounts, the Facebook Email is limited in comparison.

### What is my Facebook email address so I can give it to people?

**Jason & Kelli:**

You can only use your FB Inbox when you're logged into Facebook.

While some of the traditional features of an email account are present (Inbox, sent box, ability to compose an email, and attach Photos, Links or Videos), it is not a traditional email address that you can pass on to others outside of Facebook.

**Jason:**

To answer your question more directly, you have no Facebook email address. You just have a FB Inbox.

**Jason & Kelli:**

You can send FB Friends a message to their FB Inbox from their Profile Page or from your own FB Inbox.

When people email you through Facebook, they are sending an email to your FB Inbox. It is possible

▶▶▶

**facebook**
*and Your Marriage*

94

to compose an email and send it to as many as twenty people on Facebook and/or those with a valid email address (but they'll need a Facebook account to respond).

**Kelli:**

But like traditional email, your FB Inbox can only be accessed by you and your emails can only be read by you and those it is sent to.

## Related Threads:

- ▶ **Creating Your Own Boundaries** . . . . . . . . . . . . . . . . 341
- ▶ **Living Inbounds** . . . . . . . . . . . . . . . . . . . . . . . . . . . . . 344
- ▶ **Responding to Friends** . . . . . . . . . . . . . . . . . . . . . . . 144
- ▶ **Hiding, Removing & Blocking People** . . . . . . . . . . .191
- ▶ **Logging Into My Mate's Facebook** . . . . . . . . . . . . . 251

# About the Chat Feature

## Facebook Jargon

The Chat feature allows two FB Friends to conduct a private, real-time exchange by typing short messages to one another.

**I've never chatted before. But I see a chat function here on Facebook. How do I use it?**

### Jason & Kelli:

Chat allows two FB Friends who are both online to send short, private messages to each other in real time.

For those who are not used to chatting online, the Chat feature can be a real shock to the system. There you are, minding your own business, trolling through the pictures of another FB Friend, and BAM! A little box appears on the lower right corner of your screen with the message *"Hi! What's up?"* A few seconds later, *"Are you there?"*

Chatting can be a great way to quickly interact with one of your FB Friends who happens to be logged on to Facebook too. No one can see what you are typing, no record is kept of what is being typed, and once you log off Facebook, there is no way to recall the exchange.

This can be a function where problems can occur for marriages, especially when there is a lack of boundaries regarding who you are chatting with.

**Jason:**

There are ways to limit who can chat with you by setting up Friend Lists. Find this tip and others on chatting at **FacebookAndYourMarriage.com.**

## Related Threads:

- ▶ Setting Up Boundaries . . . . . . . . . . . . . . . . . . . . . . . . 319
- ▶ Creating Friend Lists  . . . . . . . . . . . . . . . . . . . . . . . .112
- ▶ Chatting Boundaries. . . . . . . . . . . . . . . . . . . . . . . . . 162
- ▶ Chat Responses . . . . . . . . . . . . . . . . . . . . . . . . . . . . 176
- ▶ Viewing Spouse's Chat Sessions . . . . . . . . . . . . .248

# A Note About Notes

C'mon! Join the Rest of the Planet on Facebook

## Facebook Jargon

Notes allows Facebook users to capture their own writings and share them with their FB Friends or to upload articles and information from outside of Facebook and file them in the Notes section.

## What is the Notes section for?

**Jason & Kelli:**

Notes is for you to write whatever you want and have an easy way to find it, access it, edit it, and share it with others.

**Kelli:**

The Notes section is to words what your FB Album is to pictures. With all the dynamic, real-time updates, comments, and uploads occurring, Notes allows you to create and keep something static on Facebook.

**Jason & Kelli:**

Have a poem you want to write? Want to keep your own mini-blog on Facebook? Looking to write a short story or article? Then Notes is for you. Give it a title, write something in the body, upload a picture (optional), and tag some people in the Note (also optional).

You can either Publish the Note, Preview it, Save Draft, or Discard it.

And with all things Facebook, you can tag people

▶▶▶

facebook
and Your Marriage

in the Note, share the Note with your FB Friends, or make it completely private.

**Jason:**

You can also direct RSS-feeds from your own blog, website, or other people's sites and house the updates in your Notes. Find some hints about this and other cool things you can do with Notes at **FacebookAndYourMarriage.com**.

**Jason & Kelli:**

To make the Notes easier to find, go to your Profile Page and click the + sign on the list of Tabs. In the list of options, choose Notes. It will appear as a Tab from that point forward.

## Related Threads:

- Facebook Special Features . . . . . . . . . . . . . . . . . . . . . 38
- Can a Guy Get Some Privacy? . . . . . . . . . . . . . . . . . 40
- Posting Poems and Love Notes . . . . . . . . . . . . . . . 217
- The Wall . . . . . . . . . . . . . . . . . . . . . . . . . . . . . . . . . . . . . 50
- The Profile Page . . . . . . . . . . . . . . . . . . . . . . . . . . . . . 42

# All the Fun Stuff...Applications

C'mon! Join the Rest of the Planet on Facebook

## Numbers Don't Lie

More than 500,000 active applications are currently on the Facebook Platform.

## Did You Know?

More than 250 applications have more than one million monthly active users.

## What are Applications?

### Jason & Kelli:

Applications are the "extras" offered through Facebook. Some are created by Facebook (e.g. Notes, Photos, Groups), but more are created by third-party groups.

You can go to the Applications Directory to find "extras" such as games, special features, and quizzes to add to your Facebook experience.

There is no limit to the amount of Applications you can use.

But just be careful, because a lot of the problems people have on Facebook (hacked accounts, false postings, stolen passwords) occur due to some of the third party applications.

### Kelli:

Plus, they are huge time suckers.

### Jason:

And a lot of the unspoken animosity from annoyed FB Friends occurs when we're barraged with invitations to play games, updates on games

▶▶▶

**facebook** and Your Marriage

100

people are playing, or results of trivial quizzes about trivial matters. I'm just saying.

## Facebook Jargon

Applications allow users to access games, quizzes and other special features. Some applications are created by Facebook but most are created by third-party companies.

## Related Threads:

- ▶ **A Note About Notes** . . . . . . . . . . . . . . . . . . . . . . . . . . 98
- ▶ **Quiz & Game Notifications** . . . . . . . . . . . . . . . . . . . 128
- ▶ **Sharing Pictures** . . . . . . . . . . . . . . . . . . . . . . . . . . . . 116
- ▶ **Can a Guy Get Some Privacy?** . . . . . . . . . . . . . . . . . 40
- ▶ **Spouse Spends Too Much Time on FB** . . . . . . . . . 232

# Joining Groups & Pages

## C'mon! Join the Rest of the Planet on Facebook

### Numbers Don't Lie

Pages have created more than 5.3 billion fans.

### Facebook Jargon

Pages provide a space for businesses, organizations, celebrities and brands to broadcast information, and to attract and interact with Facebook users.

## What's the difference between groups and pages and how do I join one?

### Jason & Kelli:

According to Facebook, *"Groups and Pages serve different purposes...Groups are meant to foster group discussion around a particular topic area."* *"Pages are for organizations, businesses, celebrities, and brands to broadcast great information to fans in an official, public manner."*

Groups range from the silly to the serious and there are several hundred thousand to choose from.

Some Groups are more accessible than others. An Open Group can be found through Search. To join an Open Group, click on the "Join this Group" hotlink (found right under the Group's Profile Picture). Some Groups require approval by an administrator before you can join them. And then some Groups require an invitation to join. And you cannot make a request to join an Invitation Only Group; it must be initiated by that particular Group's administrator.

To find lists of Groups, type "Groups" in the Search box and a list of initial findings will appear. Above the first listing is a drop box that features a list of different Group Types. This helps you narrow

▶▶▶

**facebook**
*and Your Marriage*

down the types of Groups you are looking for.

Once you have selected a Group Type, you'll be able to search by sub-types to further narrow your search.

**Jason:**

As you peruse different Groups and consider joining them, keep in mind that you can join no more than 300 Groups.

**Kelli:**

So choose wisely. ☺

**Jason & Kelli:**

Pages are more popular than Groups with more than one million Pages to choose from.

Once you find a Page you want to be associated with, click the "Become a Fan" link and your Facebook-based relationship with the Page is sealed.

Pages can be found in a variety of ways. You can find them through a FB Friend's recommendation, a Suggestion from Facebook, scrolling through Pages that different FB Friends are fans of (a list of Pages can be found on their Profile Page under

**Did You Know?**

Average user becomes a fan of 4 Pages each month.

**Facebook Jargon**

Groups are user developed groupings meant to foster group discussion around a particular topic area.

## Did You Know?

Average user is a member of 13 groups.

## Numbers Don't Lie

More than 20 million people become fans of Pages each day.

the Info tab), the Pages Directory, or by randomly searching names or terms in the Search box.

**Jason:**

And you'll be happy to know that you can become a fan of up to 500 Pages.

## Related Threads:

- ▶ Find-A-Friend Suggestions . . . . . . . . . . . . . . . . . . . . . 86
- ▶ Finding Help . . . . . . . . . . . . . . . . . . . . . . . . . . . . . . . . 349
- ▶ Comments — Choose Peace not War . . . . . . . . . 184
- ▶ Starting a (Facebook) Family (Group) . . . . . . . . 136
- ▶ Show `Em More Love . . . . . . . . . . . . . . . . . . . . . . . 212

*You've been a part of the social network long enough to see things that you don't know how to do or make a part of your Facebook experience. Learn how to tap Facebook for all it's worth and move from novice to expert in no time flat.*

- ▶ Custom Facebook URL .................................. 108
- ▶ SOS for Lost Friends .................................. 110
- ▶ Creating Friend Lists .................................. 112
- ▶ Making Web Links Work ............................... 114
- ▶ Sharing Pictures ...................................... 116
- ▶ Declining Friend Requests with Dignity ............... 118
- ▶ Handling Serial Facebookers .......................... 121
- ▶ What the @ Is This? .................................. 124
- ▶ Dealing with Flirts ................................... 126
- ▶ Quiz & Game Notifications ............................ 128
- ▶ Linking Your Phone & Facebook ....................... 130
- ▶ Tweeting Facebook, Facebooking Twitter .............. 132
- ▶ Starting a (Facebook) Family (Group) ................. 136
- ▶ R.I.P. My Facebook Friend ............................ 138

**Section 3**

# Let's Go! Take Your FB Experience to the Next Level

# Custom Facebook URL

Let's Go! Take Your FB Experience to the Next Level

## Transform Your Relationship

Live the Life provides relationship programs for couples before and after marriage offering WAIT Training, Adventures in Marriage, Mastering the Mysteries of Love and more. What are you waiting for?

---

**I have seen where people are able to direct people to their profile through a facebook.com/username address. How do I get one of those?**

**Jason & Kelli:**

So you want your own, exclusive Facebook web address? It's easy to get. We have one for the Facebook and Your Marriage Page (facebook.com/FBandYourMarriage).

**Jason:**

I have mine at facebook.com/marriagejunkie.

**Kelli:**

And mine is facebook.com/kellikrafsky.

**Jason & Kelli:**

Log in to your Facebook account and type in facebook.com/username in the browser address bar. (Go to **FacebookAndYourMarriage.com** if you need the visual how-to on this). Once the page loads up, you will be prompted on what to do next. Thankfully, Facebook is kind enough to let you know if the username is already taken.

▶▶▶

**facebook** and Your Marriage

108

## Custom Facebook URL

**Jason:**

Having a custom URL can make it easier for people to find you on Facebook, especially if you have a common name.

**Kelli:**

But choose wisely, you only get one chance to choose. It's kind of like a tattoo; if you don't like what you got the first time around...too bad, so sad.

### Related Threads:

- ▶ Facebook Special Features . . . . . . . . . . . . . . . . . . . . . 38
- ▶ Your BFF — Bonafide Facebook Friend . . . . . . . . . 34
- ▶ Facebook Email . . . . . . . . . . . . . . . . . . . . . . . . . . . . . . . 94
- ▶ Linking Your Phone & Facebook . . . . . . . . . . . . . . 130
- ▶ Tweeting Facebook, Facebooking Twitter . . . . . . 132

# SOS for Lost Friends

### Let's Go! Take Your FB Experience to the Next Level

**It seems like I'm missing updates from a number of my FB Friends. How do I find out if I am, and more importantly, how do I fix it?**

### Jason & Kelli:

There's nothing worse than having the feeling that something is wrong but not knowing how to fix it.

On the Home Page, Facebook allows you to determine whose updates you see and don't see in several different viewing options (including Most Recent News Feed, Top News News Feed, Status Updates and more).

### Kelli:

And there is a place to change the numbers of FB Friends' updates you see and don't. Click the "Edit Settings" link at the bottom of the Home Page and follow the prompts.

### Jason:

Because each viewing option handles this a little bit differently, you'll get a lot further a lot quicker by following the tips on this at **FacebookAndYourMarriage.com.**

▶▶▶

**facebook**
and Your Marriage

110

Let's Go! Take Your FB Experience to the Next Level

SOS for Lost Friends

**Jason & Kelli:**

Anytime Facebook makes a layout change, check the settings and make sure you're seeing all the FB Friends you want to see. This is the most common time when your FB Friends go missing or get misplaced.

## Related Threads:

- Finding Friends . . . . . . . . . . . . . . . . . . . . . . . . . . . . . 80
- Making Sense of the News Feed . . . . . . . . . . . . . . . 52
- Home Sweet Home (Page) . . . . . . . . . . . . . . . . . . . . 44
- Handling Serial Facebookers . . . . . . . . . . . . . . . . . . 121
- Hiding, Removing & Blocking People . . . . . . . . . . . 191

facebook
and Your Marriage

## Creating Friend Lists

Let's Go! Take Your FB Experience to the Next Level

### Facebook Jargon

Friend Lists allow Facebook users to manage multiple groupings of FB Friends for easier correspondence and determining levels of privacy.

My list of FB friends includes family, friends, acquaintances, co-workers, and neighbors. I don't want everyone to see everything I post. Is there a way to give certain people a certain amount of access?

**Jason & Kelli:**

The short answer is yes. But there are several steps in the process.

On the Friends page that lists all of your FB Friends, follow the prompts to "Create a List."

**Kelli:**

Your FB Friends will never know the name of the Friend List or that they are on a list at all. It is only a reference and grouping for you. Also, you can add or remove people from the lists whenever you want.

**Jason & Kelli:**

Once you have your Friend Lists, then you can go into your Privacy Settings and select which Friend Lists are not able to view certain aspects of your Facebook experience. It is an opt-out, not an opt-in privacy process.

▶▶▶

**facebook** and Your Marriage

**Jason:**

BTW, you can have up to 100 Friend Lists and up to 1,000 FB Friends on a Friend List.

**Jason & Kelli:**

Check out the mini-tutorials on setting up a Friend List at **FacebookAndYourMarriage.com**.

## Related Threads:

- Can a Guy Get Some Privacy? ................. 40
- Finding Friends ................................. 80
- Handling Serial Facebookers ................. 121
- Your BFF — Bonafide Facebook Friend ........ 34
- About the Chat Feature ...................... 96

# Making Web Links Work

Let's Go! Take Your FB Experience to the Next Level

**I write a web address in my updates but it doesn't become a live link. I've seen other people create live web links, but I can't make it work. How do I do it?**

### Jason & Kelli:

The only thing more frustrating than typing a web address into an update that doesn't hyperlink is reading an update with a web address in it that can only be viewed if it is cut-and-pasted into the browser's address bar.

We are so used to seeing URL addresses in ads that focus on the unique name of the website that we forget the most important part of any web address (and we're not talking the "w-w-w-dot"). Most of the problems with unlinked web addresses in FB Status Updates stems from neglecting to insert "http://" before the website address.

### Jason:

When updating your status or commenting on a post, if you want a URL to automatically hyperlink when you press "Share" or "Comment," then get it stuck in your head that you must type "h-t-t-p-colon-forward slash-forward slash" first.

▶▶▶

**facebook**
and Your Marriage

**Jason & Kelli:**

In the Publisher box, another way to insert a live web link is to hover the cursor over the graphic that looks like a pin in a piece of paper and click your mouse button. This will open the Insert a Link box. You can either type or cut-and-paste the URL of your choice into the box. After a few seconds, a brief explanation of the site will appear as well as the option to choose a thumbnail picture (of any applicable picture files from the linked page), and then the link is ready to be passed on to all of your FB Friends.

**Kelli:**

When inserting a link, be sure that you have a message to go with the link. Explain why you're sending it to your FB Friends and, more importantly, why they should click on the link.

## Related Threads:

- ▶ Updating Your Status..........................47
- ▶ Posting & Commenting Etiquette ..............92
- ▶ Your Friends are Hot (Linked)!.................90
- ▶ Sharing Pictures ............................116
- ▶ What the @ Is This? .........................124

# Sharing Pictures

## Let's Go! Take Your FB Experience to the Next Level

### Numbers Don't Lie

More than 3 billion photos uploaded to the Facebook site each month.

### Facebook Jargon

Photo Albums are a way for a Facebook user to group pictures in user-defined files on Facebook.

**I want to load up some pictures from our vacation. How do I get them to show up on my husband's Facebook?**

**Jason & Kelli:**

Sharing pictures with others on Facebook is so easy it hardly feels like you're sharing something.

Once you have uploaded the photos to your own Photo Album you'll have an opportunity to write a caption for each photo.

**Jason:**

And please include captions. My pet peeve is to view photos on Facebook with missing captions — no frame of reference, no names given, and no description of what I'm looking at. While it is a common human response to dread hearing people talk about their pictures (say, in a slideshow of 185 pics of your three-day vacation to Saskatchewan), most Facebookers appreciate the opportunity to read short explanations about photos they're scrolling through.

**Jason & Kelli:**

Anyway, once you have written your caption (or not), you can Tag the photo with the names of certain FB Friends by pointing the cursor on the

▶▶▶

**facebook** and Your Marriage

116

**Let's Go! Take Your FB Experience to the Next Level**

**Sharing Pictures**

picture, pushing the mouse button, and typing in their name. If they are in the picture, point on their face or body. If they're not in the picture but you want to send them the picture (say, of your kids playing a sport), click on the "Share" button and type their name. For the Tag function to work, the other person must be a FB Friend.

When people view the picture and type something in the Comment box, everyone who has been tagged will be notified of the comment.

**Jason:**

But they probably won't leave a comment if you don't write a caption! ☺

### Facebook Jargon

Tagging someone is when a Facebook user uploads a picture onto Facebook and attaches a FB Friend's name to the photo, ensuring that FB Friend is notified about the photo and has the photo placed on their Wall.

## Related Threads:

- ▸ **Can a Guy Get Some Privacy?** . . . . . . . . . . . . . . . . . .40
- ▸ **Your Profile Picture** . . . . . . . . . . . . . . . . . . . . . . . . . 74
- ▸ **Removing Bad Photos** . . . . . . . . . . . . . . . . . . . . . . 188
- ▸ **Comments — Choose Peace Not War** . . . . . . . . . . 184
- ▸ **Following the Golden Rule** . . . . . . . . . . . . . . . . . . 156

**facebook**
*and Your Marriage*

117

# Declining Friend Requests With Dignity

## Let's Go! Take Your FB Experience to the Next Level

### Transform Your Relationship

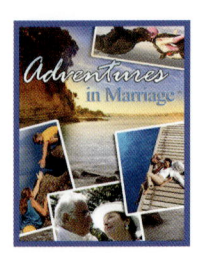

Adventures In Marriage (AIM) is an acclaimed, research-based, all-inclusive marriage education program that focuses on health, not on problems. AIM teaches specific, easy to learn skills for successful communication.

**I keep declining a friend request from someone and they keep sending a request. What can I do?**

### Jason & Kelli:

People seem to be more persistent in online communities than they are in real life. How you reject a person from entering your sacred Facebook property line depends a lot on why you want to deny their request and online friendship.

Do they not fit into your online social network? People have different reasons for being on Facebook. Some want it to be a professional network; some want it to be extremely personal; some choose to accept any and all Friend Requests and others are extremely selective. Send a brief but honest message (via the Send a Message link or by private email) to the requester explaining why you're refusing their Friend Request.

### Jason:

I had a professional colleague who sent me an email a couple of weeks after he started on Facebook. He explained that his primary reason to be on Facebook was to stay in touch with long-distance family and told me he would be Unfriending me. He apologized for the awkwardness of the situation, but valued our (professional) relationship and wanted to explain the "why." I understood and

▶▶▶

**facebook**
and Your Marriage

was fine with it. (BTW, my "100 Reasons Why I Can't Stand Scott" Facebook Group is growing members on a daily basis. Just kidding.)

### Jason & Kelli:

Is it a safety issue for you or anyone in your family? Then keep declining the Friend Request. Do not send a message to the person directly. If possible, find a mutual FB Friend you trust (by clicking on their name in the Friend Request, an abbreviated list of friends and mutual friends will appear), send a message to them, and ask if they would send a private message on your behalf to the persistent requester. In the email asking for the special favor, politely but directly ask that they stop sending Friend Requests.

### Kelli:

Facebook does have a "Permanently Decline Forever and Ever, Amen" option called Block.

### Jason & Kelli:

Is it a lack of interest in the person? There are three options for you.

First option is a fake out. Send a message to the requester saying something short and pithy like, "Wow, you're a blast from the past! Hope all is

▶▶▶

well with you!" Then click "Ignore". This will give the requester temporary access to your profile, but they'll likely get the "Whatever happened to so-and-so?" by scrolling through your profile, and once their curiosity is satisfied more than likely the desire to be FB Friends dissipates.

Second option is a give-and-go. Accept their Friend Request and then a few days later Unfriend them.

Third option is to place them on the far end of the bench. Accept their Friend Request, place them in a Friend List with extreme privacy settings, check the box to hide their updates, and more than likely you'll rarely bump into them and hardly know they're there.

So, whatever you end up doing, just remember, you are in total control of choosing your FB Friends, figuring out where to put them, and if you want, kicking them out of your Facebook life.

## Related Threads:

- Finding Friends . . . . . . . . . . . . . . . . . . . . . . . . . . . . . .80
- Hiding, Removing & Blocking People . . . . . . . . . . .191
- Friending an Ex-Spouse . . . . . . . . . . . . . . . . . . . . . 167
- Concern with Spouse Friending Exes . . . . . . . . . .242
- Spouse Overreacting on Friend Choices . . . . . . .284

Let's Go! Take Your FB Experience to the Next Level

# Handling Serial Facebookers

**A person I don't know that well sends a lot of updates each day (10-15 per day) with lengthy diatribes about their life. Is there a way to limit how many postings I get from them?**

### Jason & Kelli:

We feel your pain! Facebook is great when you get sprinkled with some details about someone's day; not so great when you get dowsed with the fine details of their life.

The first approach is the for-the-sake-of-all-Facebookers option which is to confront them. Depending on who the person is, you may feel inspired to privately inform them by email through the FB Inbox that their use of Facebook is coming across as an abuse of etiquette. Letting them know how overwhelming it is to you (and probably others) might help them tone it down a bit.

A less conspicuous, fend-for-yourself option is to Hide them from your Home Page. To Hide a FB Friend means that their postings are hidden from view on your Home Page. Hover the cursor on the top right corner of their message and the "Hide" button will appear. Click on it and you're "free at last, free at last, thank God Almighty you're free at last." Your FB Friend's updates will magically disappear, and not reappear until you say differently.

### Did You Know?

During January 2010, the average total time per person spent on Facebook was seven hours versus a little more than two hours on Yahoo and a little more than an hour on YouTube.

**facebook** and Your Marriage

Now don't worry, their posts are hidden, but not entirely lost. By scrolling down to the bottom of the page, you can click on "Edit Options" and all of the FB Friends who have been banished from the premium spot on your Home Page will magically reappear in list form with an "Add to News Feed" button.

**Jason:**

If you need a reminder of why you sequestered them in the first place, press the button, I dare you.

**Kelli:**

That's mean!

**Jason & Kelli:**

The most extreme, punish-the-guilty-perpetrator-for-clogging-up-your-Status-Update-page option is to simply Unfriend or Block them.

**Kelli:**

But if they spend that much time on Facebook to make that many Updates, they will likely notice your absence and pursue you to become a FB

Friend once again so you won't miss a moment from reading about the fine details of their life.

**Jason:**

Now that's mean! (But unfortunately spot on.)

## Related Threads:

- ▶ Home Sweet Home (Page) . . . . . . . . . . . . . . . . . . . . . .44
- ▶ Hiding, Removing & Blocking People . . . . . . . . . . .191
- ▶ Comments — Choose Peace Not War . . . . . . . . . . 184
- ▶ Following the Golden Rule . . . . . . . . . . . . . . . . . . 156
- ▶ Creating Friend Lists . . . . . . . . . . . . . . . . . . . . . . . .112

# What the @ Is This?

**Let's Go! Take Your FB Experience to the Next Level**

## Did You Know?

While Twitter has a fraction of the active users Facebook does, Twitter users post 50-million updates a day compared to Facebook users posting 60-million updates per day.

**I see some weird Updates from a few of my FB Friends. They seem to be using shorthand and referring to people and names with the @ sign in front of them. What's this about?**

**Jason & Kelli:**

Some people who use both Twitter and Facebook link the two accounts together so messages that they post on Twitter will show up on their Facebook.

Those weird updates are actually your FB Friends' Twitter messages that they have synced with their Facebook so that one update shows up in both places. You may have heard about Twitter, the popular social network where people exchange messages (called Tweets) that are 140 characters or less in length.

**Jason:**

Hence the shorthand, abbreviated messages and shortened URLs.

**Jason & Kelli:**

The @ sign with a name behind it is how people reference one another on Twitter and ensure that the person they just Tweeted will see their message. Some messages have an RT at the

▶▶▶

**facebook**
*and Your Marriage*

124

beginning which stands for Retweet and means the original Tweet is from someone else but is so good or funny or informative that it is being passed on to others.

**Jason:**

My profile name on Twitter is @marriagejunkie. If you're on Twitter, find me and follow me there.

**Kelli:**

Our Twitter profile for everything related to this book and the website is @FB_and_Marriage.

## Related Threads:

▶ The Right Amount of Updates . . . . . . . . . . . . . . . . . . 88
▶ The R.D.A. for Facebook . . . . . . . . . . . . . . . . . . . . . . 142
▶ Handling Serial Facebookers . . . . . . . . . . . . . . . . . . . 121
▶ Updating Your Status . . . . . . . . . . . . . . . . . . . . . . . . . 47
▶ Following the Golden Rule . . . . . . . . . . . . . . . . . . . . 156

# Dealing With Flirts

Let's Go! Take Your FB Experience to the Next Level

## Making a Difference

### Sexual Wholeness

Sexual Wholeness is a multifaceted, non-profit organization that promotes personal sexual integrity, positive masculinity and femininity, and passionately intimate relationships through workshops, books, articles, retreats and training.

**A FB Friend is flirting with me with comments, emails, and chats and I'm not comfortable with it at all. I'm not sure I want to be FB Friends with them anymore. What are my options?**

### Jason & Kelli:

Some people type things online they would never say in real life. Like any other social situation (a party, the workplace, a restaurant), there are social norms and etiquette we follow, and if someone crosses a line of decency, others are there to communicate the breach with their words, their gestures, and their body language.

Because being part of a social online network is so new to most Facebookers, some people haven't figured out quite where those lines of decency and mutual respect are yet.

In this situation, the first step is to talk with your spouse and let them know what is going on. Because the messages can be either public or private, others (including your spouse if he or she is on Facebook) may have read the flirting. You need to make sure your spouse knows that the flirtatious and inappropriate messages are unwanted and make you uncomfortable.

Before taking too drastic of a first step, send your FB Friend an email to their FB Inbox (and include your spouse in it) and give the person the benefit of the doubt. A message like this could work: *"Hi.*

▶▶▶

**facebook** and Your Marriage

*I don't know if you realize this but the tone of your message is flirty and makes me uncomfortable. I am happily married and would appreciate you not posting those kinds of messages. My spouse and I have also made it a habit not to chat or email with people of the opposite sex on Facebook. Thanks."*

If this gentle confrontation doesn't stop the inappropriate behavior, then Unfriend or Block the person.

**Kelli:**

But by ignoring the flirty messages and saying nothing, you're inviting it to continue, and more than likely it will increase and get more blatant.

## Related Threads:

- ▶ Should Married Facebookers Beware? . . . . . . . . . . 60
- ▶ Safeguards with Non-FB Spouse . . . . . . . . . . . . . 152
- ▶ Hiding, Removing & Blocking People . . . . . . . . . . 191
- ▶ Setting Up Boundaries . . . . . . . . . . . . . . . . . . . . . 319
- ▶ When Private Stuff Goes Public . . . . . . . . . . . . . . 186

# Quiz & Game Notifications

Let's Go! Take Your FB Experience to the Next Level

## Numbers Don't Lie

Every month, more than 70% of Facebook users engage with Platform applications.

**Some of my FB friends seem to spend a lot of time taking quizzes and their results get posted on my Profile Page. I don't care what type of drink they would be or what cartoon character they most identify with. Am I stuck having to see their results all the time?**

### Jason & Kelli:

You are preaching to the choir with this question! While we've taught our kids to replace the word "hate" with words like "greatly dislike" or "abhor," in this case we HATE Quiz notifications being posted (and receiving Gifts and getting invitations to play Games).

### Kelli:

There are even Pages devoted to rally Facebookers who share in this strong dislike on these notifications.

### Jason & Kelli:

Apparently we're not alone in this hatred, but thankfully Facebook has created an easy way to act on your annoyance and abhorrence for Quiz results as you view News Feeds.

The next time results are posted by your FB Friends, move your cursor to the right of the ▶▶▶

**facebook** and Your Marriage

128

message. A "Hide" button will appear. When you click on it, you'll be given the options to either Hide the FB Friend (which is a more permanent option, especially if they are one of those who take a lot of quizzes) or to Hide Quiz Results for that particular Quiz or results from that particular Game Application. The upside is you will never see another update for that Quiz or Application by any of your FB Friends. A mini-victory!

Unfortunately, there are hundreds and hundreds of quizzes and thousands of games and applications (and new ones being created all the time) so you will see results from these time-wasting activities you have not opted to Hide (because you haven't seen it yet). But if you Hide the results of the quizzes and applications regularly (and perhaps those FB Friends who are lured into thinking they really mean something), you will see them less often.

### Our Book Club Picks

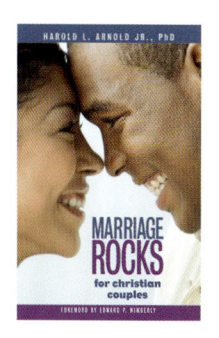

*Marriage Rocks for Christian Couples* by Harold Arnold challenges couples to establish and strengthen their relationship on a rock-solid foundation of redemption, offering, covenant, knowledge and sacred space.

### Related Threads:

- Making Sense of the News Feed . . . . . . . . . . . . . . . 52
- Hiding, Removing & Blocking People . . . . . . . . . . 191
- Handling Serial Facebookers . . . . . . . . . . . . . . . . . 121
- The R.D.A. for Facebook . . . . . . . . . . . . . . . . . . . 142
- The Right Amount of Updates . . . . . . . . . . . . . . . . 88

# Linking Your Phone & Facebook

Let's Go! Take Your FB Experience to the Next Level

## Numbers Don't Lie

There are more than 100 million active users currently accessing Facebook through their mobile devices.

**I don't have access to a computer during the day so checking my Facebook eats up my night. I heard I can access Facebook on my phone. How do I do that?**

### Jason & Kelli:

This is yet another feature that the folks at Facebook have made virtually idiot-proof. (But you can also go to **FacebookAndYourMarriage.com** for visual instructions).

Click on "Account" and then "Account Settings" and when a new screen appears with multiple tabs, choose the Mobile tab.

### Jason:

Or you can just go to the bottom of the page and in the footer, click on the term Mobile.

### Jason & Kelli:

A new window will appear that asks you to select your phone (a drop box appears with a selection of phones to choose from).

Assuming you have one of the right smart phones, Facebook will prompt you through the correct steps to make your phone talk to your Facebook account and vice versa.

▶▶▶

**facebook**
and Your Marriage

130

Let's Go! Take Your FB Experience to the Next Level

# Linking Your Phone & Facebook

**Kelli:**

Jason and I both use our iPhones to access and update our Facebook all the time. It is really easy to set up and makes accessing Facebook super convenient.

**Jason & Kelli:**

If you don't have or don't want to go through the web browser on your phone, you can also register your phone to receive notifications and update your Facebook through text messages.

**Jason:**

If you go with this option, I hope you have good rates on your texting plan.

**Did You Know?**

People that use Facebook on their mobile devices are twice as active on Facebook than non-mobile users.

## Related Threads:

- Facebook Special Features . . . . . . . . . . . . . . . . . . . . . 38
- Setting Up Boundaries . . . . . . . . . . . . . . . . . . . . . . . 319
- Mate Is Chronic Updater . . . . . . . . . . . . . . . . . . . . . 235
- Be Long Distance Lovers . . . . . . . . . . . . . . . . . . . . . 220
- Finding Solutions for Your FB Problems . . . . . . . . 328

facebook
and Your Marriage

# Tweeting Facebook, Facebooking Twitter  Let's Go! Take Your FB Experience to the Next Level

## Numbers Don't Lie

Social networking sites used by US social networkers by generation:

### Facebook:

Gen Z = 61%

Gen Y = 65%

Gen X = 76%

Boomers = 73%

WWII = 90%

### Twitter:

Gen Z = 9%

Gen Y = 14%

Gen X = 18%

Boomers = 13%

WWII = 17%

---

**I use both Facebook and Twitter. I know I can link the two so I can make one update and it shows up in both networks. I can't really see a downside to this time-saving step but want to hear what you have to say about it. So?**

### Jason & Kelli:

Before you take the plunge to merge two vastly different online social networks, think about the advantages and disadvantages of linking your Twitter and Facebook updates. While some people do this...why do *you* want to do this?

So what are the advantages?

It can save you time by having to write only one update and posting it to two different online communities. You can also spark two conversations in two places with two audiences with just one update.

### Jason:

There are several disadvantages to linking your two social networks.

One of the big differences between Twitter and Facebook has to do with the amount of updates people post in a day. It is not uncommon for someone to post dozens of updates a day on Twitter. That volume of Status Updates on

▶▶▶

## facebook
### and Your Marriage

132

Facebook on a daily basis is frowned upon, and your FB Friends will let you know that.

### Kelli:

Another disadvantage is that the Twitter-to-Facebook link is a one-lane, one-way road from Twitter to Facebook. Updates are limited to the 140 character messages on Twitter (versus 420 on Facebook), the abbreviated URL's, and the confining restrictions of Tweets. It works for Twitter because that is how Twitter is designed to function and why it is a separate social network.

But there are so many Facebook options and conveniences left on the table.

### Jason:

I have chosen not to link my Facebook and Twitter as the audiences I'm interacting with are completely different in each social network. I know personally 95 percent of my FB Friends (past and current friends, old classmates, family, business contacts, etc.).

As I look at my growing list of Twitter Followers, I know only about 3 percent to 5 percent of them personally. My purposes on Facebook are totally different from my purposes on Twitter.

**Tweeting Facebook, Facebooking Twitter**   Let's Go! Take Your FB Experience to the Next Level

### Did You Know?

In January 2010, more than 1.2 billion tweets were sent on Twitter.

### Jason & Kelli:

While it can "save time" by uploading one update for two online communities, are your audiences the same (friends and family) or different? If they're different audiences, then what you share and how you share it should probably be different. If your audiences on Twitter and Facebook are predominately the same, then choose one and stick with it.

### Jason:

As an avid Facebooker and Twitterer (is that a word?), I get annoyed by other people's Twitter messages showing up in Facebook. While I understand it is a way to "kill two birds with one stone" and saves a little bit of time, the cultures within each social network are completely different.

### Kelli:

I'm a not so avid Twitterer and seeing the RT, @ sign, and Twitter-speak on Facebook irritates the heck out of me.

**facebook** and Your Marriage

**Let's Go! Take Your FB Experience to the Next Level** — Tweeting Facebook, Facebooking Twitter

**Jason & Kelli:**

If you do end up linking them, be selective of which Tweets you send to Facebook by thinking of what would be appropriate as a two-fer update and what would not be. Also, keep track of how many you're sending over in a day. Otherwise, you might lose FB Friends over it.

**Did You Know?**

The average numbers of tweets each day:

2007: 5,000

2008: 300,000

2009: 2,500,000

2010: 39,000,000

## Related Threads:

- ▶ What the @ Is This? . . . . . . . . . . . . . . . . . . . . . . . . . . . 124
- ▶ Posting & Commenting Etiquette . . . . . . . . . . . . . . 92
- ▶ Handling Serial Facebookers . . . . . . . . . . . . . . . . . . 121
- ▶ The Right Amount of Updates . . . . . . . . . . . . . . . . 88
- ▶ Hiding, Removing & Blocking People . . . . . . . . . . 191

**facebook** and Your Marriage

# Starting a (Facebook) Family (Group)

*Let's Go! Take Your FB Experience to the Next Level*

## Numbers Don't Lie

The age breakdown of US Facebook users are:

13-17=10%

18-25=29%

26-34=23%

35-44=19%

45-54=12%

55-65=7%

**My kids are on FB and so are my husband and I. We have some other relatives that we want to share "family-only" information and pictures with. How do we do that?**

### Jason & Kelli:

Why wait one or two (or five or ten) years for the next family reunion? On Facebook, you can make everyday a family gathering! And while many of us are content to wait for the next live family get-together, families can use Facebook to connect, share family secrets, and post family photos without embarrassing the family name to the rest of the world.

The way to do this is by setting up a Group for your extended family. Facebook has made it as easy as 1-2-3 to set up a private Group page exclusively for your family members (http://www.facebook.com/family/create_group.php).

1. Establish the Group by choosing the family name that will don this Group page.

2. Invite family members who are on Facebook to join the Group.

3. Send an email to family members who are not yet on Facebook and invite them to join the family Group (and obviously Facebook too).

Then let the family fun begin!

**facebook** and Your Marriage

136

**Jason:**

And if you want to leave out the wacky uncle or the crazy aunt or the drunken grandpa, you can!

## Related Threads:

- ▶ Joining a Group or Page . . . . . . . . . . . . . . . . . . . . . 102
- ▶ Finding Friends . . . . . . . . . . . . . . . . . . . . . . . . . . . . . . 80
- ▶ Creating Friend Lists . . . . . . . . . . . . . . . . . . . . . . . . 112
- ▶ Facebook Email . . . . . . . . . . . . . . . . . . . . . . . . . . . . . 94
- ▶ Sharing Pictures . . . . . . . . . . . . . . . . . . . . . . . . . . . 116

**facebook**
*and Your Marriage*

# R.I.P. My Facebook Friend

Let's Go! Take Your FB Experience to the Next Level

## Numbers Don't Lie

The generational makeup of US internet users who maintain a social networking site profile in 2009:

Millenials
(14-26) = 77%

Gen X
(27-43) = 61%

Boomers
(44-62) = 46%

Matures
(63-75) = 36%

Total
(14-75) = 57%

**I have a friend who just died. They have a Facebook profile. Since they've passed, what will happen to their Facebook account?**

**Jason & Kelli:**

Death is one of the 100 percent guarantees in life.

**Jason:**

But if someone who has a Facebook account dies (in real life), it can be a little awkward being on Facebook and getting birthday reminders, prompts to write on their Wall or a Friend Suggestion for them.

**Jason & Kelli:**

Facebook wants to treat a person's account respectfully. Memorializing an account means that Facebook removes sensitive information and sets the privacy so that only FB Friends can see the Profile Page.

The Wall becomes a place that friends and family can leave posts in remembrance of the person. Apparently, login access becomes defunct when an account is memorialized.

▶▶▶

facebook
and Your Marriage

138

Let's Go! Take Your FB Experience to the Next Level          R.I.P. My Facebook Friend

**Kelli:**

Facebook has a form to submit so they can verify and confirm the death of the person and then memorialize their account. So suggest the next of kin to your deceased friend contact Facebook to take the steps to Memorialize their Facebook account.

## Related Threads:

- ▶ Your BFF — Bonafide Facebook Friend . . . . . . . . . 34
- ▶ The Profile Page . . . . . . . . . . . . . . . . . . . . . . . . . . . 42
- ▶ The Wall . . . . . . . . . . . . . . . . . . . . . . . . . . . . . . . . . 50
- ▶ Finding Help . . . . . . . . . . . . . . . . . . . . . . . . . . . . . 349
- ▶ Posting & Commenting Etiquette . . . . . . . . . . . . 92

**facebook** and Your Marriage

## Section 4

*Facebook doesn't cause marriage problems, people do. This thread set shares practical tips and ideas to help spouses avoid many of the problem areas and awkward situations some married people can find themselves in on Facebook.*

▶ The R.D.A. for Facebook . . . . . . . . . . . . . . . . . . . . . . . . . . . . 142
▶ Responding to Friends . . . . . . . . . . . . . . . . . . . . . . . . . . . . . . 144
▶ Password Exchange . . . . . . . . . . . . . . . . . . . . . . . . . . . . . . . . 146
▶ Avoiding FB Addiction . . . . . . . . . . . . . . . . . . . . . . . . . . . . . . 148
▶ Let Facebook Know You're Married . . . . . . . . . . . . . . . . . . . 150
▶ Safeguards with Non-FB Spouse . . . . . . . . . . . . . . . . . . . . . 152
▶ Talking FB with Non-FB Spouse . . . . . . . . . . . . . . . . . . . . . . 154
▶ Following the Golden Rule . . . . . . . . . . . . . . . . . . . . . . . . . . 156
▶ Finding Mutual Friends . . . . . . . . . . . . . . . . . . . . . . . . . . . . . 158
▶ Offensive Facebook Ads . . . . . . . . . . . . . . . . . . . . . . . . . . . . 160
▶ Chatting Boundaries . . . . . . . . . . . . . . . . . . . . . . . . . . . . . . . 162
▶ Friending Exes...or Not? . . . . . . . . . . . . . . . . . . . . . . . . . . . . 164
▶ Friending an Ex-Spouse . . . . . . . . . . . . . . . . . . . . . . . . . . . . 167
▶ Handling Embarrassing Comments . . . . . . . . . . . . . . . . . . . 170

# K.I.S.S. — Simple Ways to Safeguard Your Marriage, Your Spouse, and Yourself

# The R.D.A. for Facebook

### K.I.S.S. - Simple Ways to Safeguard Your Marriage, Your Spouse, and Yourself

## Numbers Don't Lie

50% of active users log on to Facebook in any given day.

## How much time each day should I spend on Facebook?

### Jason & Kelli:

We each have FB Friends who seem to be on Facebook all day long.

According to the Nielsen ratings, users spend an average of more than six hours a month on Facebook. This is more than any other website by a long shot.

People approach online social networks differently. Some focus on being ONLINE and spend a bulk of their Facebook time playing games, filling out quizzes, and scrolling other people's photos and reading their profiles. Some focus on being SOCIAL and use Facebook to communicate and interact with their FB Friends. Others focus on the NETWORK side of Facebook by connecting with people with shared interests or joining groups and causes that expand their influence and impact. Some people focus on all three.

### Jason:

I use Facebook professionally and personally, for SOCIAL and NETWORK purposes. Several times a

▶▶▶

## facebook
### and Your Marriage

day I spend small amounts of time on Facebook, allowing me to keep up with customers, friends, family, and my network in real time. I also use my phone to connect on Facebook, so during down time (waiting for latte, during commercials, etc) I quickly scroll through the updates of my FB Friends and view any new messages in my FB Inbox. Overall, I spend about 20-30 minutes on Facebook per day. Some days more, some days less.

### Did You Know?

The average U.S. user spent 7 hours on Facebook during the month of December 2009.

**Kelli:**

Facebook is one of the ways I stay in touch with friends down the street and across the world. I have spent up to two hours in a day on Facebook, but that is the exception, not the rule. I'm mostly on Facebook for ONLINE and SOCIAL purposes.

## Related Threads:

- Avoiding FB Addiction . . . . . . . . . . . . . . . . . . . . . . . 148
- Linking Your Phone & Facebook . . . . . . . . . . . . . . 130
- Tweeting Facebook, Facebooking Twitter . . . . . . 132
- Spouse Spends Too Much Time on FB . . . . . . . . . 232
- Mate Is Chronic Updater . . . . . . . . . . . . . . . . . . . . 235

# Responding to Friends

## Making a Difference

**FAMILYLIFE**
Help for today. Hope for tomorrow.

FamilyLife is dedicated to helping couples build healthier marriages and families though conferences, a national radio program, books, resources and more!

### Do I have to respond to all of my FB Friends' updates? There's a lot of them.

**Jason & Kelli:**

Absolutely not! Facebook has probably become so popular because we can keep informed about one another without having to interact with one another.

If we wanted to be so close to people that we interact on every detail of their lives, we would call, meet face-to-face, or send emails back and forth. But because of the constraints of time, space, and energy, we don't because we can't.

The beautiful thing about Facebook is it allows people to stay connected with one another and contact is optional.

**Jason:**

Plus, if we were obligated to type a comment for every FB Friend's update, we would be robbed of the pseudo-voyeuristic thrill that Facebook provides us. ☺

**facebook** *and Your Marriage*

144

**Jason & Kelli:**

One more thing: when you leave a comment on an FB Friend's update, you will receive a notification (via email, text message, or red notification bubble) every time someone else adds an additional comment on that same posting. If you're FB Friends with celebrities or really connected Facebookers, this can get a little obnoxious.

**Kelli:**

I learned this the hard way. I commented on someone's post and 53 other people made comments after me. That resulted in 53 emails to my regular inbox notifying me that someone commented on the post. For certain FB Friends, I now leave a related message on their Wall rather than commenting on their update.

## Related Threads:

- ▸ Posting & Commenting Etiquette . . . . . . . . . . . . . . . 92
- ▸ Handling Serial Facebookers . . . . . . . . . . . . . . . . . . 121
- ▸ Comments — Choose Peace Not War . . . . . . . . . . 184
- ▸ Sharing the Love Through Updates . . . . . . . . . . . . 208
- ▸ Creating Your Own Boundaries . . . . . . . . . . . . . . . 341

# Password Exchange

### K.I.S.S. - Simple Ways to Safeguard Your Marriage, Your Spouse, and Yourself

## Transform Your Relationship

**PREPARE/ENRICH** is a customized couple assessment completed online that identifies a couple's strength and growth areas. Based on the results, a trained facilitator provides feedback to help the couple discuss and understand their results as they are taught proven relationships skills.

---

**A friend recommended that my husband and I should give each other our FB sign-in information and passwords as a sign of full transparency and trust. Are there any rules that go along with this?**

**Jason & Kelli:**

First of all, we applaud you for doing this. We think all couples should know the user name and password to each other's profiles. This simple step can go a long way in creating mutual accountability and protecting the marriage.

But your full access pass does come with some house rules:

First, except for extreme circumstances, you shouldn't go on your mate's profile without their knowledge and permission first.

Second, if a concern or situation arises where either of you feels like you have to go on the other's profile, agree that you will talk with one another and share your concerns face-to-face.

Third, if you do go on your spouse's profile, you may not erase or delete any updates or pictures, or Block or Unfriend any of their FB Friends.

Finally, do not post any updates, send emails, or initiate or respond to chats posing as your spouse.

▶▶▶

## facebook
### and Your Marriage

## Jason:

Kelli uses my laptop sometimes to log on to her Facebook. One time, Kelli hadn't logged out so her account popped up when I tried logging into Facebook. I decided to post an update that would teasingly show her that I had been there. (It was an appropriate update, but I posed as Kelli and remarked about what a great husband I was, blah, blah, blah.) Unfortunately, three of her FB Friends commented on it before she happened to see it. I felt kind of bad about it and have never done it again.

## Kelli:

You should feel bad because you sort of graffitied my FB Wall. (But you're still a great husband!)

## Related Threads:

- ▶ Should Married Facebookers Beware? . . . . . . . . . . 60
- ▶ Logging Into My Mate's Facebook . . . . . . . . . . . . . 251
- ▶ My Spouse Is Spying on Me . . . . . . . . . . . . . . . . . . 291
- ▶ Creating Your Own Boundaries . . . . . . . . . . . . . . . 341
- ▶ Living Inbounds . . . . . . . . . . . . . . . . . . . . . . . . . . . 344

**I have an addictive-type personality when it comes to new things. I'm new to Facebook but it looks like it could be really addictive and I could spend a lot of time online. Any suggestions?**

**Jason & Kelli:**

Wow! It's good that you recognize how you're wired and are giving thoughtful concern to yourself and others before things get out of hand.

Since you know this about yourself, start a trial period for the next week or two and follow these three recommendations:

1. Find a (non-FB) Friend. This should be someone who can help you with accountability for your time online. This is someone who you've confided with, has your permission to speak into this part of your life, will be in regular communication with you, and is willing to help you succeed in keeping time boundaries with Facebook. By the way, this person should not be your spouse.

2. Set the Clock. Determine how much time per day you can spend on Facebook without jeopardizing your obligations and relationships. (Start with 15-20 minutes per day.) Set a timer (and a counselor friend of ours says it should be a kitchen timer that

you wind up). Once the alarm goes off, log out of Facebook, turn off the computer, leave the space where the computer is located, and go do something else.

3. **Write It All Down.** Journal about what you're doing on Facebook and the feelings you are having surrounding it. This provides you and your accountability partner with a written record of your Facebook experience.

At the end of the trial period, get together with your spouse and debrief about the entire experience. If you and your spouse decide to welcome Facebook into your regular routine, set similar rules as well as boundaries so Facebook is a complement to your life, not in competition with your life.

## Related Threads:

- ▸ Go on Facebook Dates . . . . . . . . . . . . . . . . . . . . . . . . 214
- ▸ Spouse Spends Too Much Time on FB . . . . . . . . . 232
- ▸ Mate Is Chronic Updater . . . . . . . . . . . . . . . . . . . . . 235
- ▸ Setting Up Boundaries . . . . . . . . . . . . . . . . . . . . . . . 319
- ▸ Finding Solutions for Your FB Problems . . . . . . . . 328

# Let Facebook Know You're Married

K.I.S.S. - Simple Ways to Safeguard Your Marriage, Your Spouse, and Yourself

## Our Book Club Picks

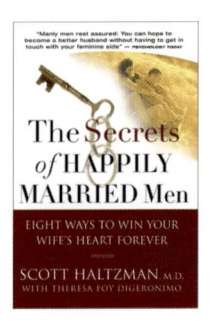

*The Secrets of Happily Married Men: Eight Ways to Win Your Wife's Heart Forever* offers practical advice for men to improve their relationships. Dr. Scott tells them that they have to understand that men and women are different and take that into account when communicating.

**I've never been a part of an online community. What can I do to make sure that people on Facebook know I'm married and not looking to "find someone."**

### Jason & Kelli:

Facebook is different from most online communities. With other online social networks, your profile can be a fake picture, a fictitious name, and a stated life that is rooted in Mr. Roger's "Land of Make Believe."

Facebook is designed to connect real people and real lives in real relationships. As with real-life relationships, one of the first things people ask about is your marital status.

When you set up your Facebook account, one of the first profile characteristics you can complete is your Relationship Status. Set it as "Married."

If your spouse is on Facebook, become FB Friends with each other and then link your relationship to "Married." This will show your FB Friends who you are married to with a live link to your spouse's Profile Page.

### Kelli:

I kind of look at setting your Relationship Status to "Married" the same as wearing a wedding ring.

▶▶▶

**facebook** and Your Marriage

150

It lets everyone know your marital status without making a big deal about it.

**Jason & Kelli:**

These next few suggestions will go beyond letting people know that you are married, and show them how married you really are.

At least once a week, make remarks about your spouse in your update. And comment on your spouse's posts fairly often. Don't be afraid to let your love show, just be sure to keep it PG-13.

Also, upload pictures of you and your spouse and store them in your Facebook Photo Album. Write descriptions on the photos and link your spouse on them. That way, anytime someone comments on the pictures, you and your spouse will receive a notification about it. At times, choose a picture of you and your spouse as your Profile Picture.

## Related Threads:

- Joint or Solo Account?. . . . . . . . . . . . . . . . . . . . . . . . .68
- Maiden or Married Name?. . . . . . . . . . . . . . . . . . . . .72
- Relationship Status. . . . . . . . . . . . . . . . . . . . . . . . . . .76
- Sharing the Love Through Updates. . . . . . . . . . . .208
- Special Moment Shout-Outs. . . . . . . . . . . . . . . . . .222

## Making a Difference

Family Builders Ministries provides opportunities and tools that couples, parents, and those who minister to them can use in building great marriages and families from generation to generation.

### My husband isn't on Facebook, so what can I do to "safeguard" my marriage?

### Jason & Kelli:

Great question! Just because your husband isn't connected on Facebook doesn't mean he can't connect with you about Facebook. (How's that for a triple negative?)

First, talk with him. It is on you to initiate a conversation with your spouse about the kinds of things you are doing on Facebook (connecting with friends, sharing photos, playing games, etc.). Ask him if he has any questions or concerns about Facebook or your activities on the social network. Don't get defensive or annoyed at the questions (or lack of questions) that come up. Validate him and any interest he may show.

Second, discuss boundaries with him. It's important for you to come prepared with ones you're setting and to ask if he would like you to set others. Boundaries set clear lines for mutual accountability and fairness in the relationship. This conversation (or series of conversations) can alleviate resentments and jealousy, especially when your mate doesn't have a shared interest in Facebook.

Third, update him about your Facebook experience. Be sensitive to how much or how little information he is interested in. The important thing is to keep the communication flowing so if an issue does come up there is already open and honest dialogue occurring.

**Kelli:**

And make sure that your Relationship Status is marked as "Married."

**Jason:**

And write something about him from time to time in your updates.

## Related Threads:

- ▸ Talking FB with Non-FB Spouse . . . . . . . . . . . . . . . . 154
- ▸ Loving a Non-FB Spouse on Facebook . . . . . . . . 204
- ▸ The "About Us" Date . . . . . . . . . . . . . . . . . . . . . . . . . 334
- ▸ Creating Your Own Boundaries . . . . . . . . . . . . . . . . 341
- ▸ Living Inbounds . . . . . . . . . . . . . . . . . . . . . . . . . . . . . 344

# Talking FB With Non-FB Spouse

**K.I.S.S. - Simple Ways to Safeguard Your Marriage, Your Spouse, and Yourself**

## Transform Your Relationship

The Flag Page is an effective way to get your spouse to tell you how they feel – all without them saying a word! The five minute online program is so easy, positive and non-threatening, because it measures one thing: passion — what you truly love the most about life.

**My wife isn't on Facebook but asks questions about all my FB Friends. Is she paranoid or something?**

### Jason & Kelli:

It's doubtful your wife is suffering from an emotional or mental ailment if your recent Facebook activity has triggered your alarm bells for the first time.

It seems that you're annoyed or irritated by her interest in your FB experience. You should really be honored by her questions, because more than likely she's feeling a little left out and is trying to connect with you about something that gives you some fun and pleasure.

Whether she's intimidated by technology or unsure about being a part of a social network, it seems fair that she would have some questions about something her husband is spending time doing. In fact, you should really worry if she stops asking questions.

Talk with her and find out why she isn't on Facebook. She may be waiting for an invitation. If she is intimidated by Facebook, let her sit next to you a few times when you log on and show her what she's missing out on. Show her what's on your Profile Page and as you scroll around, let her know what your personal boundaries are.

**facebook** *and Your Marriage*

**Jason:**

If she's still not interested in joining Facebook, make your life easier and your relationship less stressful- man up and engage her on this. And don't wait for her to ask the questions either. When you log off, talk with her and share who you've been connecting with, people you're reconnecting with, funny posts you've read, pictures of mutual friends, whatever. Otherwise, you could have more serious issues than just misdiagnosing your wife's metal health.

**Kelli:**

In a lot of ways, your Facebook account is a lot like a scrap book. It has a bunch of people, pictures and information that all have something in common...you. What wife wouldn't want to know what's in her husband's scrap book?

## Related Threads:

- ▸ Safeguards with Non-FB Spouse . . . . . . . . . . . . . . 152
- ▸ Starting Up on Facebook. . . . . . . . . . . . . . . . . . . . . 70
- ▸ Setting Up Boundaries . . . . . . . . . . . . . . . . . . . . . . 319
- ▸ Go on Facebook Dates . . . . . . . . . . . . . . . . . . . . . . 214
- ▸ Talking Without Fighting . . . . . . . . . . . . . . . . . . . . 314

# Following the Golden Rule

**K.I.S.S. - Simple Ways to Safeguard Your Marriage, Your Spouse, and Yourself**

## Making a Difference

**Formacion Matrimonial**

Formacion Matrimonial is reaching the Hispanic community throughout Central California with relationship skills training, marriage education and fatherhood programming.

**My husband and I just got in an argument and he said some hurtful things to me. I am tempted to get back at him by writing something on my status update. What do you think?**

### Jason & Kelli:

What's the universal response to a toddler running into a busy street? No! Don't! Stop! All of the above.

This same series of knee-jerk reactions is appropriate for this situation.

Facebook is a great way to communicate with old and new friends, and a tremendous way to interact with your spouse. But your Facebook updates are not the place to "get back" at anyone, especially your spouse.

### Jason:

I cringe anytime I see a spouse "get back," go off on, or put down their mate on Facebook. It's a sure sign that there are some bigger problems in the relationship, and unfortunately they've brought their FB Friends into the middle of it. Thank you very much.

▶▶▶

**facebook**
*and Your Marriage*

156

**Kelli:**

I live by what we call the Golden Rule of Facebook: "Publicly post stuff about others in the same way you would want them to post stuff about you." This goes for updates, postings on Walls, and commenting on photos, videos, links, or other posts.

**Jason & Kelli:**

Overall, if you can't Facebook something nice, you shouldn't Facebook anything at all.

## Related Threads:

- Posting & Commenting Etiquette . . . . . . . . . . . . . . 92
- Hiding, Removing & Blocking People . . . . . . . . . . .191
- Sharing the Love Through Updates. . . . . . . . . . .208
- Resolving Conflict Quickly . . . . . . . . . . . . . . . . . .322
- Calling for an "About Us" Date. . . . . . . . . . . . . . .338

# Finding Mutual Friends

**K.I.S.S. - Simple Ways to Safeguard Your Marriage, Your Spouse, and Yourself**

## Making a Difference

**Marriage Network OKLAHOMA**

Marriage Network Oklahoma is a group of faith based organizations whose goal is to provide a network of information about how couples can build strong marriages, and the resources to make it happen.

**How can I find out who my husband and I share as friends on Facebook? Also, I'd like to send our friends invites to parties and special updates about our family without informing all the other people on Facebook. Is there a way to set up groups of friends?**

### Jason & Kelli:

Discovering the FB Friends you and your husband have in common is really easy. Log into your Facebook account and go to his Profile Page. A group of photos under the heading "Mutual Friends" appears and allows you to go view them.

If you want to ensure that each of you has as many mutual FB Friends as possible, scroll through each other's full list of FB Friends. If you see someone on his list that is missing on yours, you can send a Friend Request right then and there.

Once you both have had a chance to do this, now you can set up a Friend List of your shared FB Friends and email messages to them from the FB Inbox, easily Tag them, or Share with them anything you're posting on Facebook.

**facebook**
*and Your Marriage*

158

**Jason:**

You could also set up a private Group with the whole group of FB Friends but that would only work if they know each other. Regardless of what you end up doing, there's help for you at **FacebookAndYourMarriage.com**.

**Kelli:**

I love your idea! It's almost like having a personal Christmas card list on Facebook, but rather than sending them something once a year, you can keep them more informed and up to date all throughout the year!

## Related Threads:

- Finding Friends . . . . . . . . . . . . . . . . . . . . . . . . . . . . . 80
- Friend Swap with Spouse? . . . . . . . . . . . . . . . . . . . . 82
- Creating Friend Lists . . . . . . . . . . . . . . . . . . . . . . . . 112
- Declining Friend Requests with Dignity . . . . . . . . 118
- Hiding, Removing & Blocking People . . . . . . . . . . 191

# Offensive Facebook Ads

## Transform Your Relationship

**I.N.F.O.**
imperfect.normal.families.only.

I.N.F.O. for Families is a blog designed to help regular families stay informed, equipped and on task. With articles ranging from marriage helps, parenting tips and family issues, this site is for imperfect, normal families only.

---

**There are some Facebook ads that are kind of risqué with girls in underwear with the headline that someone is looking for me. I'm happily married and not interested. What can I do to complain about the ad?**

### Jason & Kelli:

There's some good news and bad news related to ads on Facebook.

First, the good news. Facebook has created a way for people to switch out ads. The steps on this action are found at **FacebookAndYourMarriage.com**.

Now for the bad news. Removing the ad is only a temporary fix and that particular ad will likely reappear.

### Kelli:

If you're really offended with the ads, contact Facebook's advertising department and request a more permanent solution.

Who knows if it will work, but at least your gripes will be read and recorded. The more Facebook hears from its members on what is and is not acceptable, they may make some changes.

▶▶▶

**facebook** and Your Marriage

160

**Jason:**

And sometimes letting our grievances be known can make all the difference...in our own minds at least.

## Related Threads:

- ▶ Should Married Facebookers Beware? . . . . . . . . . . 60
- ▶ Is Facebook Evil? . . . . . . . . . . . . . . . . . . . . . . . . . . . 58
- ▶ Finding Help . . . . . . . . . . . . . . . . . . . . . . . . . . . . . 349
- ▶ Setting Up Boundaries . . . . . . . . . . . . . . . . . . . . . 319
- ▶ Creating Your Own Boundaries . . . . . . . . . . . . . . 341

# Chatting Boundaries

**K.I.S.S. - Simple Ways to Safeguard Your Marriage, Your Spouse, and Yourself**

## Our Book Club Picks

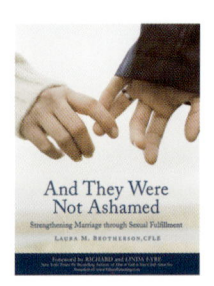

*And They Were Not Ashamed* by Laura Brotherson is a book providing comprehensive, in-depth, and respectfully reverent information about physical intimacy and marital oneness.

**I feel uncomfortable chatting with people, but don't want to come across rude. What can I do?**

### Jason & Kelli:

There is a more pressing question: Have you and your spouse discussed what is and is not acceptable with using Chat? Chats are private, non-recorded sessions between the two people involved in the chat exchange. Upon logging out, the contents of the chat session are erased forever.

How do you and your spouse feel about non-public correspondence with people of the opposite sex? This is a necessary discussion for couples to have. It may be that your discomfort is linked to your uncertainty about where you as a couple stand on the issue.

### Kelli:

This is a definite area on Facebook where couples need shared and agreed upon boundaries. For Jason and me, we've decided not to chat with people of the opposite sex. But there are situations that come up where we feel compelled to respond to a chat. Afterwards, we tell each other about it and what was chatted about. It's our way of keeping open lines of communication.

### facebook
*and Your Marriage*

162

# K.I.S.S. - Simple Ways to Safeguard Your Marriage, Your Spouse, and Yourself

## Chatting Boundaries

**Jason:**

I dread the little bell ringing and the little window popping up with an uninvited FB Friend writing, "Hi! How are you?" Sometimes it is welcome, but other times you just don't feel like being social.

**Kelli:**

Boo to you! I don't mind it a bit!

**Jason & Kelli:**

Unexpected chat sessions can create some anxiety. But unwanted chat sessions can be really uncomfortable. The easy answer... turn off the Chat feature or restrict those who can see the green dot indicating that you are on-line. (The action steps to this tip are at **FacebookAndYourMarriage.com**.)

### Related Threads:

- ▶ **About the Chat Feature** . . . . . . . . . . . . . . . . . . . . . . . . . . 96
- ▶ **Creating Friend Lists** . . . . . . . . . . . . . . . . . . . . . . . . . . 112
- ▶ **Dealing With Flirts** . . . . . . . . . . . . . . . . . . . . . . . . . 126
- ▶ **Chatting Boundaries** . . . . . . . . . . . . . . . . . . . . . . . . 162
- ▶ **Setting Up Boundaries** . . . . . . . . . . . . . . . . . . . . . . . 319

**facebook** and Your Marriage

# Friending Exes...or Not?

**K.I.S.S. - Simple Ways to Safeguard Your Marriage, Your Spouse, and Yourself**

## Making a Difference

The California Healthy Marriages Coalition offers relationship and marriage education classes for singles and couples all throughout the Golden State in different settings, languages and formats.

**Our school reunion is coming up. I signed up for FB and friended a lot of people from high school and a few of them were ex-girlfriends. I would love to find out what's going on in their lives, but I think my wife would totally freak out. Should I do it and not tell her, or should I just forget about it?**

### Jason & Kelli:

It sounds like your conscience is talking to you. And you're kind of listening. But it sounds like you're wavering a bit.

So let's think about this. If you were to reach out to your exes and your wife was not to find out, what would be the best case scenario? You find out about their lives? You stroll down memory lane? You reignite a relationship of some kind?

Now, let's say you connect with your exes and don't tell your wife. What could be the worst case scenario if she were to find out? Would she yell at you, be upset with you, give you the silent treatment, leave you, or throw you out?

### Kelli:

And realize that her finding out is pretty likely. If she were to stroll through your FB Friends list, see a comment on your update, or view a posting

▶▶▶

## facebook
### and Your Marriage

164

on your Wall by one if not all of your exes, you'll be found out.

### Jason & Kelli:

Or, if you were to become FB Friends with them, would she not mind or give it a second thought? The fact that you're worried that she would "freak out" indicates that you know her reaction will be one of the options listed in the worst case scenario.

### Jason:

Since you've been listening to your gut on this, you need to turn to the voice of your wife.

### Jason & Kelli:

Before you have that conversation, think about why you want to reconnect with your old flames. Think about your motives, your hopes, and your desires. Then talk to her and find out what she thinks. You may be surprised. You may confirm your suspicions. But it's better to have the conversation on this side of sending or accepting the Friend Requests.

# Friending Exes...or Not?

### K.I.S.S. - Simple Ways to Safeguard Your Marriage, Your Spouse, and Yourself

**Kelli:**

Jason and I have had a number of discussions about this very issue after we realized that we both had people from our past in our group of FB Friends. We determined that since there's no real benefit to our marriage for either of us to reconnect with people we've dated in the past, we decided to Unfriend the ones in our list of FB Friends and decline Friend Requests from any former love interests.

## Related Threads:

- ▶ **Declining Friend Requests with Dignity** . . . . . . . . .118
- ▶ **Friend Requests from Old Flames** . . . . . . . . . . . . 179
- ▶ **Hiding, Removing & Blocking People** . . . . . . . . . .191
- ▶ **Ex's Profile Pic Sparks Feelings** . . . . . . . . . . . . . .282
- ▶ **Talking Without Fighting** . . . . . . . . . . . . . . . . . . . 314

# K.I.S.S. - Simple Ways to Safeguard Your Marriage, Your Spouse, and Yourself

# Friending an Ex-Spouse

**My ex-husband (and the father of my two kids) is on FB. I am now remarried and starting a new life. My kids say I should be FB Friends with my ex. What do you think?**

### Jason & Kelli:

There are some pros and cons to being FB Friends with the other biological parent of your kids. And there are some definite rules to follow and boundaries to set for you, your ex, and your kids (assuming they're on Facebook).

But first, you need to think about why this would or could be advantageous. This could be a way for the kids to link with both of their parents and for them to stay in better contact with both their mother and father. Depending on custody issues, Facebook could provide an avenue to reduce conflict and animosity surrounding the exchange of kids for custodial visits. It also allows both parents to stay a little more connected with the kids when they're with the other parent.

Once you've determined whether it would make life easier or more difficult (because there is nowhere to hide once you're linked together in a social network), then a conversation with your current spouse is essential. You can make the case for it, but ultimately your spouse needs to be OK with the idea.

**Transform Your Relationship**

## hitched

Hitched is an online magazine that provides informative articles, helpful resources and interactive experiences aimed at entertaining, educating and inspiring marriages.

▶▶▶

**facebook** and Your Marriage

And with a few firm boundaries in place, any fears they have should be alleviated. The boundaries need to be shared with the kids and the ex, and they're non-negotiable.

First, all correspondence on Facebook between you and the ex must be public (posts on each other's Walls, comment on updates, or leaving comments on photos only). No messages through Chat or FB Inbox.

Second, all public dialogue on Facebook must be civil, respectful, and solely about the kids. No put downs, cutting comments, or disclosure of private details should be tolerated.

Third, neither of you is allowed to comment on each other's posts that share personal life issues, such as dating, personal choices, etc.

Finally, by no means should the kids or the ex write anything about the parents getting back together.

### Jason:

In some cases it may be better to Hide each other's posts so neither one of you has to regularly read the updates of the other. Writing on each other's Wall and tagging photos should suffice and avoid any blurring of the lines between shared parenting and personal lives.

**Kelli:**

And it's probably a good idea for your current spouse to be a FB Friend with your ex too.

## Related Threads:

- Hiding, Removing & Blocking People . . . . . . . . . . .191
- Posting & Commenting Etiquette . . . . . . . . . . . . . .92
- Comments — Choose Peace Not War . . . . . . . . . 184
- Sharing Pictures . . . . . . . . . . . . . . . . . . . . . . . . . .116
- Setting Up Boundaries . . . . . . . . . . . . . . . . . . . . 319

# Handling Embarrassing Comments

## K.I.S.S. — Simple Ways to Safeguard Your Marriage, Your Spouse, and Yourself

### Making a Difference

**National Fatherhood Initiative**

The National Fatherhood Initiative provides all kinds of resources to help men become more responsible fathers, more engaged husbands, and better dads. The group behind many of the most popular fatherhood public service announcement campaigns gives fathers everything they need to know to be a great dad.

---

**My wife writes really affectionate and intimate things on my wall and in her comments on my status. I'm not a real lovey-dovey kind of guy and her comments, while appreciated, are a bit embarrassing. How do I tell her to tone it down without hurting her feelings?**

### Jason & Kelli:

What are you worried about? Are you embarrassed that others may be reading it, or are you being teased by friends?

Before making this an issue with her, think about your wife: Why is she doing this? What is her intent in doing this? Is she trying to embarrass you or show you some tender loving care?

More than likely, one of her most comfortable ways of showing you her love is to express it with words. If so, she is giving you one of the greatest gestures of love she knows how to give.

If you end up addressing the matter with her, tread lightly. First, let her know how much you appreciate her and how she expresses her love to you. And then give her alternatives to express herself to you privately on Facebook (such as sending messages through Chat or the FB Inbox).

▶▶▶

**facebook** and Your Marriage

170

**Kelli:**

Let me give you some woman's advice here. Your wife would LOVE to be on the receiving end of a written message of how much you love her. Since this comes so naturally to her, it is likely the best way for you to speak to her heart.

**Jason:**

Dude, listen to my wife. She knows what she's talking about!

## Related Threads:

- Facebook Email ................................. 94
- About the Chat Feature ......................... 96
- Sharing the Love Through Updates ............ 208
- The "About Us" Date .......................... 334
- Calling for an "About Us" Date ................ 338

*The biggest challenge of being a part of the world's largest sub-culture is not knowing how to handle unpredictable situations and unexpected correspondences. Get the inside scoop on how to expect the unexpected and what to do when it occurs (and it will).*

▸ **Getting Poked** . . . . . . . . . . . . . . . . . . . . . . . . . . . . . . . . . . 174
▸ **Chat Responses** . . . . . . . . . . . . . . . . . . . . . . . . . . . . . . . . 176
▸ **Friend Requests from Old Flames** . . . . . . . . . . . . . . . . 179
▸ **International Friend Requests**. . . . . . . . . . . . . . . . . . . . . 182
▸ **Comments — Choose Peace Not War** . . . . . . . . . . . . . . . 184
▸ **When Private Stuff Goes Public** . . . . . . . . . . . . . . . . . . . 186
▸ **Removing Bad Photos** . . . . . . . . . . . . . . . . . . . . . . . . . . . 188
▸ **Hiding, Removing & Blocking People** . . . . . . . . . . . . . . .191
▸ **Something Seems Phishy**. . . . . . . . . . . . . . . . . . . . . . . . . 194
▸ **Is Message Legit or a Scam?**. . . . . . . . . . . . . . . . . . . . . . 196
▸ **Reducing Activities Reporting** . . . . . . . . . . . . . . . . . . . . 198
▸ **Closing Facebook Account** . . . . . . . . . . . . . . . . . . . . . . .200

**Section 5**

# Surprise! How to Expect the Unexpected and Not Sweat It

# Getting Poked

## It's Been Said

*(The poke feature) "is the digital equivalent of waving at someone from across a crowded room."*

ABC News

**Someone just poked me. Not sure if I should be offended or honored. What does it mean?**

### Jason & Kelli:

The Poke feature is to Facebook what tonsils are to your body. At some point it probably had meaning and importance, but it really serves no meaningful purpose now.

Poking someone (or being poked) is a way for a FB Friend to let another FB Friend know they're there and just saying "Hey!" That's all it is.

### Jason:

I got poked once when I first got on Facebook. When I sent my FB Friend a message to find out what it meant, he wrote back that he didn't realize he had done it and didn't know what it meant. My only poking on Facebook was a false poke. How pathetic is that?

### Kelli:

I poked someone once and they poked me back. I don't really see a reason for it. If I want to get in touch with someone, I view the list of my FB Friends who are online, and if I want to say

▶▶▶

# Surprise! How to Expect the Unexpected and Not Sweat It

## Getting Poked

something, I either use Chat or write something on their Wall.

**Jason & Kelli:**

So, what we're saying is don't worry about getting poked or poking others. It seldom happens because most people don't use the Poke feature.

### Facebook Jargon

The Poke feature is a way for one Facebook user to get the attention of another Facebook user.

## Related Threads:

- ▶ The Wall . . . . . . . . . . . . . . . . . . . . . . . . . . . . . . . . . . . 50
- ▶ Facebook Special Features . . . . . . . . . . . . . . . . . . . . 38
- ▶ About the Chat Feature . . . . . . . . . . . . . . . . . . . . . . 96
- ▶ Posting & Commenting Etiquette . . . . . . . . . . . . . . 92
- ▶ Chatting Boundaries . . . . . . . . . . . . . . . . . . . . . . . . 162

**facebook** and Your Marriage

# Chat Responses

## Surprise! How to Expect the Unexpected and Not Sweat It

**Yikes! Someone just popped up in my Chat box. I felt like I had to chat with them but didn't want to. What can I do?**

### Jason & Kelli:

On Facebook, you don't have to do anything you don't want to do.

Surveying some (real-life) friends about chatting, people's reactions range from excitement to drudgery with underlining resentment due to feeling obliged to converse with someone at an inconvenient time.

If your phone rings, you can let it go to voicemail. The caller doesn't know you have the cordless phone in your hand, you're reading the Caller I.D., and have elected not to answer the phone. They assume you didn't hear the phone.

With Facebook, the little green dot gives it away that you're logged into the social network. So if it's not a convenient time to chat, or you're in the middle of something else, or you simply don't want to chat, what are your options?

### Jason:

Here are three sure-fire ways to ignore and avoid chatting. I know because I do all three. First, ignore the invitation to chat. Even though your

▶▶▶

facebook *and Your Marriage*

176

dot is green, it doesn't mean you're actively on Facebook at that moment. Your FB Friend will likely think you've just stepped away from your computer.

Another option is to close out the Chat pop-up window by clicking on the "X" in the top right corner. This is the step above plus removing the pesky miniature window. However, if the FB Friend types another chat message, the window pops-up again.

If you know that you have no interest in chatting (or want to prevent the Chat pop-up window from ever appearing), turn off the Chat feature by clicking on "Options" and then click "Go Offline" at the top of the newly opened box. This will keep you online but makes it appear to others that you are offline.

### Kelli:

If you want to be more civil and polite, here are a couple of alternatives to "Jason the Hermit's Anti-Chatting Tips." (Love you, Honey!)

### Jason & Kelli:

First, you can blow them off without blowing them off. Send a message like this: "Hi, I'm in the middle of something and can't chat right now.

Have a good one!" This acknowledges them but allows you to keep doing what you're doing.

Or, if chatting has not been a part of your online experience, give it a try for a week or two and see if you like it.

**Kelli:**

If not, then you can try one of Jason's tips above.

**Jason:**

See you in two weeks! Just don't try to chat with me to let me know you've chosen to turn off your Chat feature.

## Related Threads:

- ▶ Chatting Boundaries..........................162
- ▶ About the Chat Feature.......................96
- ▶ Posting & Commenting Etiquette..............92
- ▶ Following the Golden Rule...................156
- ▶ Viewing Spouse's Chat Sessions..............248

# Friend Requests from Old Flames

## I just got a friend invite from an old flame. What do I do?

### Jason & Kelli:

What would your spouse want you to do? Don't know? Then before you press the "Accept" button, have a discussion (and perhaps a series of discussions) with your spouse about becoming FB Friends with past boyfriends/girlfriends (and throw into the mix anyone you have been romantically or physically involved with, had a strong crush on, or dated).

Facebook attempts to connect people who have some kind of common past. It also allows you to search for people from the past. It has no way of knowing what kind of connection you had or to weigh the potential impact that relationship could have on your present and future. You're the filter, not Facebook.

This situation will come up for both of you (many times), so it is up to you (and your spouse) to determine the type of people each of you is comfortable re-establishing a relationship with via Facebook.

As you two determine where the boundary lines of comfort and discomfort are, each of you needs to honor the other's convictions and feelings, and

### Did You Know?

"Nancy Kalish, author of the book, *Lost & Found Lovers: Facts and Fantasies of Rekindled Romance*, says that most people are looking for these lost loves fairly innocently, just for curiosity…If the person sought out online is a past love from the adolescent years, that may be the greatest risk."

▶▶▶

**facebook** and Your Marriage

then draw the line at the same spot. If one of you is comfortable with becoming FB Friends with old love interests and the other one is not, then neither of you should friend them.

### Jason:

We had been on Facebook for several months before Kelli and I had this very discussion. After talking it through, we decided not to be FB Friends with people we had had any sort of an intimate or emotional past with. When a Friend Request does come in from someone who meets that criteria, before clicking "Ignore", I send a message like this: "Hey, thanks for the friend request. Some time back, my wife and I talked and decided that neither of us would connect with past partners or love interests on Facebook. So in honor of my wife and marriage, I'm not able to accept your Friend Request. I hope you understand and don't take it personally. I wish you the best for your life! Best, Jason."

### Kelli:

At the time of our discussion, we both had people from our past that were FB Friends. But when we decided they no longer fit within our new, agreed upon boundaries, Jason and I both Unfriended them.

Surprise! How to Expect the Unexpected and Not Sweat It

Friend Requests from Old Flames

**Jason & Kelli:**

If for some reason you both decide that you're OK with not setting limits on who you become FB Friends with, then keep this as an open discussion topic that could change in time.

**Jason:**

And be sure to set boundaries on the ways you do and do not communicate with your old flames.

## Related Threads:

- Declining Friend Requests with Dignity . . . . . . . . .118
- Concerns with Spouse Friending Exes . . . . . . . . .242
- Make Past Boy/Girlfriend a Current FB Friend? . .280
- The "About Us" Date . . . . . . . . . . . . . . . . . . . . . .334
- Creating Your Own Boundaries . . . . . . . . . . . . . . 341

**facebook** and Your Marriage

# International Friend Requests

**Did You Know?**

There are more than 70 language translations available on the Facebook site.

**How cool! Someone from India wants to be my friend. Is it OK to accept friend requests from people you don't know?**

**Jason & Kelli:**

Sure! And be sure to tell your children that strangers always give out the best tasting candy.

Remember learning about "stranger danger" as a kid? While you don't have to be worried about getting abducted or kidnapped, you should be highly concerned about identity theft. It's really difficult to trace and prosecute identity theft domestically. When it happens internationally, it is virtually impossible to resolve.

Facebook can be a safe place when you know your FB Friends and they are really friends (and family). When you start accepting Friend Requests from acquaintances, strangers, or people you would like to get to know...everything changes.

Remember, your FB Friends can see everything you post unless you use the Privacy Settings.

**Kelli:**

The old adage, "It's better to be safe than sorry," applies here. If you don't know the person, ignore the friend request.

# Surprise! How to Expect the Unexpected and Not Sweat It

# International Friend Requests

### Jason & Kelli:

If they send another Friend Request, click on their name and view their profile. Do you share any mutual FB Friends? Can you see any information or details on their Profile Page that gives you a reason to accept their Friend Request?

As a last resort, you could send them a message asking why they want to be friends. But it is important to know that when you send the message, they will gain temporary access to view your Profile Page.

### Jason:

Save yourself the time and stress, click "Ignore", and get back to your FB Friends. You know, the people you actually know and who know you.

### Did You Know?

About 70% of Facebook users are outside the United States.

## Related Threads:

- ▶ Finding Friends . . . . . . . . . . . . . . . . . . . . . . . . . . . . . 80
- ▶ Declining Friend Requests with Dignity . . . . . . . . . 118
- ▶ Creating Friend Lists . . . . . . . . . . . . . . . . . . . . . . . . 112
- ▶ Handling Friend Requests . . . . . . . . . . . . . . . . . . . . 84
- ▶ Hiding, Removing & Blocking People . . . . . . . . . . . 191

**facebook** and Your Marriage

# Comments — Choose Peace Not War

## It's Been Said

*"Actually I think this is one of the most profound changes that more openness and transparency brings: It puts more weight and importance on building better social relationships and being more trustworthy."*

Mark Zuckerberg, Facebook Co-founder

---

**A FB Friend just posted a political comment I totally disagree with. I really want to write a comment back but I'm not sure if I should. What say you?**

### Jason & Kelli:

The only thing that is more awkward than reading a public online spat is being involved in one.

Think about it, all the necessary (and helpful) elements of a live, face-to-face confrontation are absent when an online exchange occurs. You can't read body language and facial expressions. You can't hear tone of voice. You can't easily detect sarcasm or tongue-in-cheek comments. You don't know if the other person is reading your words and thoughtfully considering your feelings.

### Jason:

And then you have the ever present "troll" who finds great joy in stirring up things with outrageous statements just to view people's online reactions.

### Jason & Kelli:

What you may view as a civil exchange of differing viewpoints can easily erupt into a mini melodrama ▶▶▶

---

**facebook** *and Your Marriage*

184

## Surprise! How to Expect the Unexpected and Not Sweat It

## Comments — Choose Peace Not War

that sucks up a lot more time and energy than you imagined.

**Kelli:**

I've seen my fair share of posting and comment exchanges that have blown up way out of proportion.

**Jason:**

If you are really passionate about the issue and want to share your perspective with someone, do it privately using your FB Inbox or call them on the phone.

### Facebook Jargon

Comment is a way for FB Friends to respond to what another FB Friend has posted, whether it is an update, a picture, a link or anything else.

## Related Threads:

- ▶ Updating Your Status . . . . . . . . . . . . . . . . . . . . . . . . . 47
- ▶ Making Sense of the News Feed . . . . . . . . . . . . . . . 52
- ▶ Following the Golden Rule . . . . . . . . . . . . . . . . . . . 156
- ▶ Handling Embarrassing Comments . . . . . . . . . . . 170
- ▶ When Private Stuff Goes Public . . . . . . . . . . . . . . . 186

**facebook**
and Your Marriage

# When Private Stuff Goes Public

### Surprise! How to Expect the Unexpected and Not Sweat It

## It's Been Said

*"Please keep in mind that if you disclose personal information in your profile or when posting comments, messages, photos, videos...this information may become publicly available."*

Facebook

---

**Someone just wrote something on my Wall that shouldn't have been a public message. I don't want others to read it. How do I get rid of it?**

### Jason & Kelli:

First things first, getting rid of the message is easy. Go to your Wall and hover the cursor to the right of the message. A little "Remove" button will appear. Click on it and the message will magically disappear.

For newbies on Facebook, it takes a little time for people to get the hang of how Facebook works, including appropriate and inappropriate places to post certain messages.

We recommend sending that person a message through the FB Inbox. Explain how Facebook works and the difference between comments on a Wall versus comments on a posting versus sending an email through the FB Inbox. Let them know that those kinds of messages are better reserved for private viewing instead of public broadcasting.

### Jason:

Give them the benefit of the doubt that they were acting in ignorance instead of stupidity. More than likely, they'll appreciate the coaching.

▶▶▶

**facebook** *and Your Marriage*

**Jason & Kelli:**

Unfortunately, there is a good chance that some of your FB Friends read the message on their Home Page. You need to determine if there is anyone (possibly mentioned or referred to in the post) that needs to be apologized to. Send that person a private message through the FB Inbox and let them know how you addressed the issue with the message originator, distance yourself from the comment, and apologize for the situation.

**Kelli:**

And don't forget to fill your spouse in on the matter too.

## Related Threads:

- ▶ The Wall . . . . . . . . . . . . . . . . . . . . . . . . . . . . . . . . . . . . . . . . 50
- ▶ Posting & Commenting Etiquette . . . . . . . . . . . . . . . 92
- ▶ Handling Embarrassing Comments . . . . . . . . . . . . 170
- ▶ Hiding, Removing & Blocking People . . . . . . . . . . . 191
- ▶ Facebook Email . . . . . . . . . . . . . . . . . . . . . . . . . . . . . . . 94

# Removing Bad Photos

Surprise! How to Expect the Unexpected and Not Sweat It

## Making a Difference

Family Frameworks is dedicated to creating healthy marriages and reducing the divorce rate by serving as a resource to offer accessible information and exceptional programming.

**An old friend posted some photos from college that shows me with my ex-girlfriend. It's something I don't really want others to see, especially my wife. What can I do to block the photo?**

### Jason & Kelli:

There's some good news, some kinda-good news, and some bad news.

The good news is that you can remove the picture from your Profile Page. In fact there are two ways to do this. First is to remove the Tag. Click on the photo and when the page with the photo comes up, click on the "Remove Tag" link and it will be removed from your Profile Page. You can also go to your Wall, hover the cursor to the right corner of the post and a "Remove" button will appear. Click on it and the picture will disappear.

### Jason:

If you need more specifics on how to do this, go to **FacebookAndYourMarriage.com**.

### Jason & Kelli:

The kinda-good news is that it is possible for the photo to be removed from Facebook...as long as the person who posted it will remove it.

▶▶▶

**facebook**
*and Your Marriage*

Send the person an email through your FB Inbox (or for quicker action, see if they're online and use the Chat feature, or for even more immediate action, call them). Explain that the photo is something you don't want posted on Facebook and request that they remove it.

### Jason:

Depending on the person, you may have to do a little begging and pleading as the "I don't want my wife to see the picture" excuse may not be enough to motivate them to remove the photo.

### Jason & Kelli:

Now for the bad news. Since the photo was posted and tagged with your name (and possibly others who are in the picture or others tagged for tagging sake), the photo got posted on each person's Wall, showed up on each person's Home Page, and likely showed up on the Photos Page on your FB Friends (and their FB Friends) Home Pages.

So if your spouse is on Facebook, there is a very good chance that she has seen it, will see it, or will hear about it. As much as you want to hide this from your wife, you are better off informing her as soon as possible about the photo. But share with her about all you've done to remove it from your Profile Page and from Facebook altogether.

▶▶▶

**Kelli:**

The sooner you can inform your wife on the picture, the better. It will lessen the emotional impact if she does see it.

## Related Threads:

- The Wall . . . . . . . . . . . . . . . . . . . . . . . . . . . . . . . . . . . . . . . .50
- Posting & Commenting Etiquette . . . . . . . . . . . . . . .92
- Handling Embarrassing Comments . . . . . . . . . . . . 170
- Sharing Pictures . . . . . . . . . . . . . . . . . . . . . . . . . . . . .116
- Calling for an "About Us" Date . . . . . . . . . . . . . . . .338

# Hiding, Removing & Blocking People

**I friended an ex-boyfriend and have realized that it was a really bad idea to do so. What can I do to remove him?**

**Jason & Kelli:**

There are times when it would be nice if we could remove people from our real lives as easy as it is to remove a FB Friend on Facebook. Whether the person is a family member, an obnoxious acquaintance or an ex-boyfriend, Facebook gives you three options to deal with them.

**Jason:**

To make it easy, all three of the options below are explained and shown in greater detail at **FacebookAndYourMarriage.com**.

**Jason & Kelli:**

If you don't want to totally remove the person from your Facebook life, but don't want to see their regular updates, you can Hide them. On your Home Page, hover the cursor to the right of their update. When the "Hide" button appears, click on it and you won't see their postings again. They are still a FB Friend, so you can still message them and they can message you (using

## Transform Your Relationship

Laugh Your Way to a Better Marriage is a marriage conference like no other. Between laughs, learn relationship tips and marriage insights guaranteed to stick with you for a long time! Attend a conference in a public venue or in the privacy of your own home. Either way, your marriage will never be the same!

▶▶▶

**facebook**
*and Your Marriage*

## Facebook Jargon

Hide is an option for Facebook users to remove the posts and updates from a particular FB Friend from their own Home Page, but still keeps the FB Friend and allows for correspondence.

## Facebook Jargon

Unfriending someone is when one Facebook user removes another Facebook user as a FB Friend and therefore, both users will no longer see updates from each other.

FB Inbox or Chat or posting a comment on each other's Wall).

The second option is to Unfriend them. Go to their Profile Page and click on the "Remove from Friends" link. This step removes them from being one of your FB Friends, and removes you from being one of their FB Friends. While you're not viewing their posts, comments and updates, they will show up in Friend Suggestions and in Friend Searches.

The third (and most extreme) option is to Block the FB Friend. This step is taken through your Privacy Settings. When you Block someone, they are not able to find or view your account on Facebook. You won't be able to view their account either. You are virtually invisible to one another.

**Kelli:**

When you Block someone, it is totally confidential. They don't get a notice or anything; you just disappear from their Facebook experience.

**Jason:**

If for some reason you want to become FB Friends with a person you've put a Block on, then you will need to Unblock them and send a Friend Request.

### Jason & Kelli:

You'll need to come up with your own criteria and reasoning when you apply the different levels of distancing yourself from people on Facebook. Why Hide someone? What type of FB Friend do you Unfriend? When do you Block someone?

Our advice with ex-boyfriends and ex-girlfriends (and anyone else who has touched your heart) is to either Unfriend them or Block them altogether.

### Kelli:

And as soon as possible, make this a topic of conversation with your spouse to make sure you both are on the same page when it comes to exes.

### Facebook Jargon

Blocking someone is when one Facebook user removes another Facebook user as a FB Friend and neither Facebook user will be visible to each other on Facebook.

## Related Threads:

- Dealing with Flirts............................126
- Friending Exes or Not?......................164
- Friend Requests from Old Flames.............179
- Handling Embarrassing Comments..............170
- Calling for an "About Us" Date...............338

# Something Seems Phishy

## Surprise! How to Expect the Unexpected and Not Sweat It

### Did You Know?

Facebook has created "complex automated systems that detect compromised accounts." If an account is sending out an unusually high volume of messages to friends, the account is frozen."

---

**I just got a FB Email from a friend saying they have a photo of me from a trip and that I should check it out. I've never been on a trip with them. Did they send it to me by mistake?**

### Jason & Kelli:

Click on the link and it will be at least a week and hundreds of dollars in computer services before you see your computer operate properly again. This is a virus of lethal proportions.

### Kelli:

We've had a number of FB Friends who have clicked on the link. It is so sad that these kinds of viruses can be on Facebook. So beware!

### Jason & Kelli:

Phishing is a practice where bad guys try to trick people into sharing their user name and password. Never trust something that sounds phishy, smells phishy, or looks phishy. Whatever it may be or how convincing it may sound, it is always better to delete it and be wrong than to open it up and pay dearly.

Not only do the phishing scams send messages to your FB Inbox, but also postings to your

Wall that say things like, "Your Profile Picture is on such-and-such website" or "Check out this video." Sometimes the name of the messenger is someone you don't know, and sometimes it is one of your FB Friends.

**Jason:**

If you do recognize the name of the person who sent you the message, that means their user name and password were stolen to find other FB Friends who will click the link and submit their username and password, so....

## Related Threads:

- ▶ Can a Guy Get Some Privacy? . . . . . . . . . . . . . . . . . .40
- ▶ Removing Bad Photos . . . . . . . . . . . . . . . . . . . . . . . 188
- ▶ Facebook Email . . . . . . . . . . . . . . . . . . . . . . . . . . . . .94
- ▶ Hiding, Removing & Blocking People . . . . . . . . . . .191
- ▶ Is Message Legit or a Scam? . . . . . . . . . . . . . . . . . . 196

# Is Message Legit or a Scam?

## Our Book Club Picks

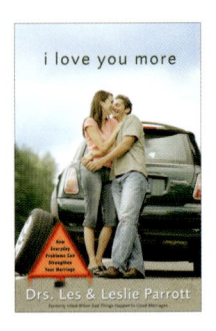

*I Love You More* provides the secrets to using everyday problems to strengthen your marriage. Explore how a marriage survives and thrives when a couple learns to use problems to boost their love life and to literally love each other more.

**I got an email from a friend of mine who is stuck in Europe and needs some cash. It seems a little fishy. Should I delete it or head down to Western Union to transfer some money?**

### Jason & Kelli:

Fact one, your friend is not in Europe. Fact two, if they are in Europe, they aren't stuck there. Fact three, if they were stuck in Europe, they wouldn't contact you at a crisis moment. Fact four, if your friend would contact you at a crisis moment while in Europe, Facebook is not the means by which they would choose to do so.

This is one of several phishing scams that has made its way into the Inboxes of lots of Facebookers. While more realistic sounding than the prime minister of Nigeria contacting you to transfer his $14 million to your bank account for safekeeping, it is just another way scammers are attempting to extract information and money from unsuspecting and gullible people.

Your first option is your best…just delete it.

### Jason:

Hopefully the day will never come when I really am stuck in Europe and need money and Facebook is my only way to communicate with friends and family. That'd be a real bummer.

▶▶▶

**facebook**
*and Your Marriage*

196

**Jason & Kelli:**

You may also find emails in your regular inbox that look like they're from Facebook with subject lines ranging from "login security" to "change your password." There is a hotlink within the body of the email to take care of the "urgent" issue. This, too, is a scam to get you to enter your vital information so the bad guys can take it from you.

**Kelli:**

Anytime Facebook wants you to do something, there will be a message when you securely log in to your Facebook account.

## Related Threads:

- ▶ Can a Guy Get Some Privacy? . . . . . . . . . . . . . . . . . 40
- ▶ Responding to Friends . . . . . . . . . . . . . . . . . . . . . . . 144
- ▶ Facebook Email . . . . . . . . . . . . . . . . . . . . . . . . . . . . . 94
- ▶ Something Seems Phishy . . . . . . . . . . . . . . . . . . . . 194
- ▶ International Friend Request . . . . . . . . . . . . . . . . . 182

**facebook**
*and Your Marriage*

# Reducing Activities Reporting

*Surprise! How to Expect the Unexpected and Not Sweat It*

## Making a Difference

Friends of the Family Ministries is a non-profit, non-denominational organization committed to building healthy relationships by providing a variety of services including counseling, workshops and seminars, teaching and coaching.

**I feel like I have a GPS attached to my every move on Facebook. Everything I do seems to be recorded on my Wall. Is it possible to stop the tracking?**

### Jason & Kelli:

You do have some controls on what is posted about what you do on Facebook. And, you can determine who can or cannot view the details of your Facebook experience. But it won't make you completely invisible. Some of your actions will still be recorded on your Wall.

Go to the Privacy Settings and begin making the changes you want. If you are really concerned with what people can see, start extreme by making very little visible to others. Over time, loosen up on the settings as you feel comfortable.

### Kelli:

It is kind of weird to have almost everything you do on Facebook recorded on your Wall and in your FB Friends' News Feed.

### Jason:

There are all kinds of options to change the recording of your Facebook activities.

▶▶▶

**facebook**
*and Your Marriage*

We have laid out the steps with visuals at **FacebookAndYourMarriage.com**.

■

## Related Threads:

▶ Can a Guy Get Some Privacy? . . . . . . . . . . . . . . . . . 40
▶ The Wall . . . . . . . . . . . . . . . . . . . . . . . . . . . . . . . . . . . 50
▶ Making Sense of the News Feed . . . . . . . . . . . . . . . 52
▶ Home Sweet Home (Page) . . . . . . . . . . . . . . . . . . . . 44
▶ When Private Stuff Goes Public . . . . . . . . . . . . . . . 186

# Closing a Facebook Account

### I need to close down my Facebook account. How do I do this?

**Jason & Kelli:**

Do you want to take a break for awhile or disappear for good?

You can Deactivate your Profile, which basically means that your account becomes inaccessible to your FB Friends. This is a perfect option if you're going on a temporary hiatus.

**Jason:**

It's kind of the same thing as having the post office hold your mail while you're gone on vacation.

**Jason & Kelli:**

You can Reactivate your account at any time with your FB Friends, your Photos, your Privacy Settings, and everything else fully intact.

The more extreme step is to Delete your account. This will completely remove and delete your account and any and all of your information.

▶▶▶

**Kelli:**

Consider what you really want to do long-term. If you think you will one day return to Facebook, it is probably a good idea to Deactivate your account. And if in time you think that your Facebook days are over, you can log back in and Delete your account.

## Related Threads:

- Comparing Online Social Networks............36
- Facebook Special Features...................38
- Fad or Fixture?.............................56
- Should Married Facebookers Beware?..........60
- Setting Up Boundaries......................319

## Section 6

*Spouses have a new tool in their cache to romance their loved one...Facebook. This set of threads is filled with flirty ideas and romantic suggestions to utilize Facebook as another way to express love to one's mate and regularly woo your spouse.*

- ▶ Loving a Non-FB Spouse on Facebook ............... 204
- ▶ Sharing the Love Through Updates .................. 208
- ▶ Flirting on Facebook ................................. 210
- ▶ Show `Em More Love ................................ 212
- ▶ Go on Facebook Dates .............................. 214
- ▶ Posting Poems & Love Notes ....................... 217
- ▶ Be Long Distance Lovers ........................... 220
- ▶ Special Moment Shout-Outs ........................ 222
- ▶ Creative Invites to Date Your Mate ................. 224
- ▶ The Ultimate Surprise .............................. 226

# Let's Get It On! Have a Facebook Affair...With Your Spouse!

## Transform Your Relationship

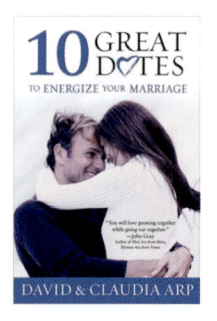

10 Great Dates will help you reclaim that same spark, connection, and creativity in your marriage through ten intentional, memory-making dates. This proven approach to relationship growth is low-key, purposeful, effective, easy, and fun.

---

**I feel like I'm missing out. I see a lot of my married friends flirting with and saying beautiful things to their husbands on Facebook. What can I do if my husband isn't on Facebook?**

### Jason & Kelli:

Facebook has definitely opened some new opportunities for husbands and wives to share the love with their mate. And while communicating with your hubby through Facebook is difficult if he's not a part of the online community, it's not impossible.

### Kelli:

There are several things you can do for your husband and your marriage regardless if he ever starts an account.

### Jason & Kelli:

First thing, since your husband is unknown on Facebook, make sure the Facebook community knows about him. Be sure your Relationship Status is set to "Married."

Next, upload a photo of the two of you and make it your Profile Picture. After that, upload a bunch more pictures of the two of you (and pictures of

▶▶▶

204

the kids and family too) into one or more Photo Albums. Be sure to comment on the pictures and refer to your husband in every one he is in.

When you update your status, on a somewhat regular basis, refer to your husband by sharing specifically what you appreciate about him and what you love about him. Give updates when he does special things for you and when you have special dates with him planned.

Over time, word will get back to him about what you're posting. Friends and family will ask about certain events, activities or situations you wrote about. He will feel like a hero as they shower him with praise (by people infected by the praise you're heaping on him on Facebook).

### Kelli:

Who knows, he may join Facebook because people keep telling him of all the sweet and kind words you're writing about him.

### Jason & Kelli:

But don't just sit around hoping that one of your FB Friends shares what you're posting about him, show him yourself. You can print a screen shot of your Wall or you can have him sit next to you as you show off your Wall, your Profile Page and your

Photo Album. At the very least, it will show him that you're thinking about him and your marriage while you're on Facebook.

### Jason:

And that may help alleviate any anxiety of fears he hasn't shared with you about your being on Facebook.

### Jason & Kelli:

Also, keep your husband informed on who you are becoming FB Friends with whether he seems interested or not. It is vital to keep the communication lines open about your Facebook experience whether he joins in on the fun or stays on the sidelines.

### Kelli:

One more thing, you can email him from Facebook. Send photos, links or whatever else to his regular email so at least he can get a peek-a-boo view into what you're enjoying on Facebook.

**Jason:**

The main point is to make him as much a part of your Facebook experience as you possibly can. It's not as easy if he's not on Facebook, but it is still possible.

## Related Threads:

- Safeguards with Non-FB Spouse . . . . . . . . . . . . . . 152
- Talking FB with Non-FB Spouse . . . . . . . . . . . . . . . 154
- Let Facebook Know You're Married . . . . . . . . . . . 150
- Go on Facebook Dates . . . . . . . . . . . . . . . . . . . . . 214
- Setting Up Boundaries . . . . . . . . . . . . . . . . . . . . . 319

# Sharing the Love Through Updates

## Making a Difference

**Better Marriages**
Educating Couples · Building Relationships

Better Marriages educates couples for vibrant, lifelong relationships through a variety of workshop and seminar formats. Formerly known as the Association for Couples in Marriage Enrichment, Better Marriages is one of the oldest marriage strengthening organizations in the country.

**I never know what to write about my wife when I update my status. Can you give me some pointers?**

### Jason & Kelli:

Relax! An update is much like a casual greeting or small talk with someone. Stop over-thinking it!

Think about significant dates (first date, got engaged, wedding, special moments) in your relationship and reference it in a posting ("Ten years ago today I asked my wife to marry me and thankfully she said yes.")

On the rest of the 350-360 days that may not have a special moment attached to them, share specifically what you love about her or what you appreciate about her. Thank her for amazing acts of love and sacrifice that she shows to you ("I love that my wife has my coffee ready for my commute to work every morning. Her doing that is more of an energy boost than my cup of Joe.")

Don't feel like you have to say something about her every day. But do try to post something about her in your updates once every week or so.

### Jason:

Personally, I love it when Kelli references me in her updates.

▶▶▶

**facebook** and Your Marriage

Let's Get It On! Have a Facebook Affair...With Your Spouse!

Sharing the Love Through Updates

### Jason & Kelli:

When it comes to writing something about your wife, keep in mind that she will read it. Whatever you write, just make sure it is something that she'll appreciate and not embarrass her.

And, if you want to write something a little more private, or make it more personal, write something on her Wall, or if it's really private, send an email through the FB Inbox.

### Kelli:

When Jason is away on business trips, almost every morning he writes something on my Wall. I love that!

## Related Threads:

- ▶ The Right Amount of Updates . . . . . . . . . . . . . . . . . 88
- ▶ Posting & Commenting Etiquette . . . . . . . . . . . . . 92
- ▶ Facebook Email . . . . . . . . . . . . . . . . . . . . . . . . . . . . . 94
- ▶ Special Moment Shout-Outs . . . . . . . . . . . . . . . . . 222
- ▶ Posting Poems & Love Notes . . . . . . . . . . . . . . . . 217

**facebook**
and Your Marriage

209

# Flirting on Facebook

Let's Get It On! Have a Facebook Affair...With Your Spouse!

## Making a Difference

**BUILDING INTIMATE MARRIAGES**

Building Intimate Marriages seeks to help individuals learn the skills for them to sustain a committed, satisfying, intimate marriage with their spouse. They accomplish this through professional marriage therapy, a variety of workshops and various resources for couples and individuals.

**I want to flirt with my wife, but I don't want people to see what I write on her Wall. What can I do?**

**Jason & Kelli:**

Thank you for thinking of others. We don't mind seeing words of affection between spouses, but we don't want to read things that make us feel like we need to take a cold shower.

**Jason:**

It's the equivalent of being in a public place and seeing a couple give each other a quick kiss on the lips versus having to watch a couple make out.

**Jason & Kelli:**

There are two ways to communicate with your wife in the "dimly lit corners" and "private rooms" of Facebook.

If she is online on Facebook at the same time as you, try the Chat feature. No one can see the real-time exchange of words, and there is no saved record of your words. Get as risqué and flirty as you feel comfortable with no worries.

▶▶▶

**facebook** and Your Marriage

**Kelli:**

Just make sure you close down the Chat box and/or log out of Facebook when you're done; especially if you're using a public or family computer. Otherwise, the Chat box may be left open for others to read.

**Jason & Kelli:**

If she is not online on Facebook at the same time as you, send her an email message through the FB Inbox. When she logs in to Facebook, she'll see you left her a message and will be able to read it, save it, and reread it again and again.

Different from Chat, your email messages will save both the message you sent and the one she hopefully sends back to you. ☺

## Related Threads:

- ▶ About the Chat Feature . . . . . . . . . . . . . . . . . . . . . . 96
- ▶ Facebook Email . . . . . . . . . . . . . . . . . . . . . . . . . . . . . 94
- ▶ Chatting Boundaries . . . . . . . . . . . . . . . . . . . . . . . 162
- ▶ Posting Poems & Love Notes . . . . . . . . . . . . . . . . 217
- ▶ Show `Em More Love . . . . . . . . . . . . . . . . . . . . . . 212

# Show 'Em More Love

Let's Get It On! Have a Facebook Affair...With Your Spouse!

## Transform Your Relationship

**Radical Love**

Radical Love offers a unique approach to marriage fully woven in scripture that will both challenge and inspire couples in relating to God and each other. Marriage is explored as the epitome of the Christian experience and encourages couples to examine their own relationship in this manner. An eye-opening, jaw dropping experience that equips couples to connect with their whole heart!

**Besides writing on his Wall, posting updates, sending him a message or chatting with him through Facebook, what else can I do to show love to my husband?**

**Jason & Kelli:**

Love your enthusiasm to move beyond the basics!

**Jason:**

The first and (in my opinion) worst idea is to send him FB Gifts that are available on Facebook. These little pictures have as much meaning, value, and appreciation as the stuffed animals you win at a carnival. I personally hate the stuff, but others seem to like it.

**Jason & Kelli:**

One possibility is to set up a Photo Album devoted to your relationship. Fill it with all kinds of photos of the two of you. Tag him in the photos and write something schmaltzy in the comment section. Keep in mind that when you're writing the comments, the photos can be viewed by your FB Friends and possibly others.

Another idea is to write something on your blog or website (if you have one) and then send him the URL link for that page.

▶▶▶

**facebook** and Your Marriage

This final idea is a little extreme. Start a Page that's all about him. (Steps to build a Page are at **FacebookAndYourMarriage.com**.) Build it around a theme — his next birthday, his interests, or his good looks. Invite other people to "Become a Fan" to help bombard your husband with affirmation.

For a little more privacy, set up a private Group. Invite only him to join the Group and you two will have your own sacred space on Facebook.

**Jason:**

Hey Kel, why don't you set up one of those private Group pages for us?

**Kelli:**

Yeah, I'll be sure to get right on that.

## Related Threads:

- ▸ All the Fun Stuff...Applications . . . . . . . . . . . . . . . . 100
- ▸ Making Web Links Work . . . . . . . . . . . . . . . . . . . . 114
- ▸ Sharing Pictures . . . . . . . . . . . . . . . . . . . . . . . . . . . 116
- ▸ Joining Groups & Pages . . . . . . . . . . . . . . . . . . . . . 102
- ▸ Posting Poems & Love Notes . . . . . . . . . . . . . . . . 217

## Making a Difference

**Living Well** empowers men and women to discover the true living well through addressing the principles of growth and adjustment in marriage and family development.

**I am having such a great time going down memory lane on Facebook. I'm realizing that there are whole parts of my life that my wife doesn't know about (friends, experiences) that I want to tell her about. How do you suggest I do that?**

### Jason & Kelli:

Sounds like a great time to set up a Facebook date.

This is where you and your wife spend some time at the computer or on your smart phone together and scroll through each other's FB Friends and their pictures. Grab a glass of something, dim the lights, and spend some time sharing the memories.

Be sure to share how you met certain people, tell stories you remember about that person, and why this person was (or wasn't) significant in your life.

### Kelli:

Now, this doesn't all have to be done in one sitting. Each of you can take turns "introducing" the other to your old classmates (say from elementary to high school), people from your hometown, family members, whoever. Stick with a theme or a segment of your life and get more mileage out of traipsing down memory lane.

### Jason & Kelli:

And you don't have to make it all about the past. This can be a great way to talk about FB Friends who are part of your current life (like co-workers, people your spouse doesn't know, etc).

### Jason:

And if you want to make the time a little more productive, you could create Friend Lists since you'll already be clustering your friends into logical groupings.

### Kelli:

Are you serious? Trying to be "productive" during a date? Really?

### Jason:

Ummm...no, I was just making a joke.

**Jason & Kelli:**

And if you get through all your FB Friends, share the Groups and Pages you've joined on Facebook. Why did you join them? How did you find out about them? What kinds of updates do they send and why is it important to you?

The key is that you and your spouse are talking about your Facebook experiences and connections and having your own experience and connection together.

## Related Threads:

- ▶ Your BFF — Bonafide Facebook Friend . . . . . . . . . 34
- ▶ Joining Groups & Pages . . . . . . . . . . . . . . . . . . . . . 102
- ▶ Creating Friend Lists . . . . . . . . . . . . . . . . . . . . . . . 112
- ▶ Concerns with Spouse Friending Exes . . . . . . . . 242
- ▶ Living Inbounds . . . . . . . . . . . . . . . . . . . . . . . . . . . 344

Let's Get It On! Have a Facebook
Affair...With Your Spouse!

# Posting Poems & Love Notes

**The box to type updates into is too small for me to post my poems for my wife. Is there somewhere else I can post these?**

### Jason & Kelli:

The 420-character limit of the Publisher Box (where you type your updates) is a real bummer for the more verbose among us.

There are two ways to capture your love poems (or love letters or private notes) in full and share them with your wife using Facebook.

The first is in Notes. You can type your poems and determine the Privacy Settings (who can view them).

The other way to share your "love captured in words" with the missus is to post them on a blog or a website (hosted outside of Facebook) and then post the URL link to your wife's Wall or send it to her in a message she accesses in her FB Inbox.

### Kelli:

Either way, the poems are saved in as permanent a place as possible on Facebook.

## Transform Your Relationship

**TwoOfUs.org**

TwoofUs.org is an online clearinghouse designed to provide couples with the information, the resources, and the help they need to make their relationship better. Whether you're dating, engaged or married, there is something for you!

**facebook**
and Your Marriage

# Posting Poems & Love Notes

**Jason:**

Or you could get into writing those short poems. What do they call them? Origami?

**Kelli:**

Origami is Japanese paper folding.

**Jason:**

What's the name for those short poems where you can only use a certain amount of words?

**Kelli:**

It's called Haiku. LOL

**Jason:**

Yeah, take up Haiku and then you can definitely fit your poems into the Publisher Box.

**Jason & Kelli:**

Facebook can handle all of your written expressions of love no matter how long or how short they are. If you're poetic or not, if you want to make your writing private or public, if you're writing them using Facebook's features or not... Facebook has you covered."

## Related Threads:

- ▶ Can a Guy Get Some Privacy? ................40
- ▶ The Wall .....................................50
- ▶ Facebook Email ..............................94
- ▶ A Note About Notes ..........................98
- ▶ The Ultimate Surprise .......................226

# Be Long Distance Lovers

### Let's Get It On! Have a Facebook Affair...With Your Spouse!

**Both my husband and I work and we're on Facebook at different times (and sometimes different time zones when he travels). How can we use Facebook to "get it on"?**

### Jason & Kelli:

Yowzers!

There are plenty of ways for a husband and wife to (cue the Barry White music now) "get it on" on Facebook, whether you're across the room, across the country, or across the world.

The Wall is a natural place to post morning greetings and nighttime goodnights. By writing on each other's Wall, each of you has something to look forward to when logging into Facebook.

### Kelli:

Just be sure not to make it too obvious that either of you is away. It can be a security issue for sure.

### Jason & Kelli:

Uploading photos through the Publisher Box (where you write your update) can be a great way to share in your experiences while miles apart. Tag your husband on the photo so he's sure to see it.

▶▶▶

**facebook** and Your Marriage

**Kelli:**

You can each join Groups of unashamed spouses. There are plenty of Groups to post your lovey-dovey comments in a spot where they won't seem out of place, but they'll find great company with other adoring marrieds sharing amorous words about their spouse.

**Jason:**

Or you could set up a private Group for just the two of you.

**Kelli:**

Then let the "getting it on" get it on.

## Related Threads:

- Posting & Commenting Etiquette . . . . . . . . . . . . . . 92
- Joining Groups & Pages . . . . . . . . . . . . . . . . . . . . . 102
- Sharing Pictures . . . . . . . . . . . . . . . . . . . . . . . . . . . 116
- Sharing the Love Through Updates . . . . . . . . . . . 208
- Show `Em More Love . . . . . . . . . . . . . . . . . . . . . . . 212

# Special Moment Shout-Outs

Let's Get It On! Have a Facebook Affair...With Your Spouse!

## Making a Difference

**Marriage Resource Center** of Miami Valley

Marriage Resource Center has developed initiatives that build value and awareness for healthy relationships and marriages as well as provides marriage and relationship education.

---

**My wife and I have been on Facebook for about six months. Our 13th anniversary is coming up next week. What could I do on Facebook to celebrate our anniversary?**

**Jason & Kelli:**

You've got good instincts. Your wife will love that (1) you remembered your anniversary, (2) you made your anniversary greetings public, and (3) many FB Friends are celebrating your anniversary too.

**Jason:**

And the funny thing is, it really doesn't take that much effort to make a big splash about your anniversary on Facebook.

**Jason & Kelli:**

First, on the morning of your anniversary, write something nice on her Wall.

Next, post an update announcing to all your FB Friends that it is your anniversary. Hotlink her name in the post and she'll be sure to see it.

Finally, post a wedding picture on your Wall and write an endearing comment about your wedding day. Don't forget to Tag her in the photo.

▶▶▶

**facebook** and Your Marriage

**Kelli:**

This will be an anniversary your wife will always remember. While it's the 13th you celebrate together, it's your first to be celebrated on Facebook. Awwww!

**Jason:**

Keep these tips in mind for other significant dates such as, when you first met, when you first kissed, the day you got engaged and other major milestones.

**Kelli:**

Birthdays and Mother's Day are no-brainers.

## Related Threads:

- The Wall . . . . . . . . . . . . . . . . . . . . . . . . . . . . . . . . . . .50
- Your Friends are Hot (Linked!) . . . . . . . . . . . . . . . . . .90
- Sharing Pictures . . . . . . . . . . . . . . . . . . . . . . . . . . . .116
- All the Fun Stuff...Applications . . . . . . . . . . . . . . . .100
- Show `Em More Love . . . . . . . . . . . . . . . . . . . . . . . 212

**facebook**
*and Your Marriage*

# Creative Invites to Date Your Mate

## Transform Your Relationship

*Intentional Moments*

Intentional Moments purpose and passion is to inspire friendship, renew commitment and rekindle romance between husbands and wives.

**I have this great idea! My husband and I take turns planning our date nights. I want to send him the details for our next date using Facebook. What are different ways I can use Facebook to send him an invite?**

**Jason & Kelli:**

That is a great idea. Depending on how much time and creativity you want to spend on this invite, there are several ways to use Facebook as your own personal Mr. Postman.

The easiest (and least creative ways) are: posting a general invite on his Wall, sending the date specifics in a message to his FB Inbox, or use the Chat feature when both of you are on Facebook and send him the specifics on your date.

The Event feature is a great way to plan events and send invites to as many FB Friends as you want, to a party, meeting, conference, or a private gathering. Go to the Home Page and find the Event icon. Click on it and follow the prompts to fill in the details of the event (your date night). Be sure to make the Privacy Setting either Closed or Secret and when it comes to sending the invite, make sure you only send it to him. You have the opportunity to make the Event as creative and specific as you want it to be.

▶▶▶

**facebook** and Your Marriage

**Jason:**

Another idea is to take a picture of a handwritten note detailing the specifics of the date, upload it onto Facebook, and tag him. It will show up on his Wall.

**Kelli:**

Create a visual scavenger hunt with cropped pictures or pieces of the date details (time, location, etc) and over the course of a week, send the photo to his FB Inbox that gives him hints of what is coming his way. It builds a little bit of suspense and intrigue for your date night.

## Related Threads:

- Facebook Email . . . . . . . . . . . . . . . . . . . . . . . . . . . . .94
- Can a Guy Get Some Privacy? . . . . . . . . . . . . . . . . .40
- The Wall . . . . . . . . . . . . . . . . . . . . . . . . . . . . . . . . . . .50
- Sharing Pictures . . . . . . . . . . . . . . . . . . . . . . . . . . .116
- The Ultimate Surprise . . . . . . . . . . . . . . . . . . . . . . .226

# The Ultimate Surprise

*Let's Get It On! Have a Facebook Affair...With Your Spouse!*

## Transform Your Relationship

www.MARRIAGEjunkie.com

Ramblings of a Marriage Junkie is the regular fix for those committed to reviving marriage & reducing divorce - in their own home and in their own community! This blog features articles on social media's impact on relationships and other current trends impacting marriages today.

**I want to do something for my husband on Facebook that is over-the-top. Suggestions?**

### Jason & Kelli:

OK. This idea is truly over-the-top and not for the faint of heart. The multi-step process to make it happen takes a modest amount of planning.

### Jason:

But it will likely result in a showering of love and appreciation upon you that you have rarely experienced in this lifetime. (Yeah, a bit of an embellishment but you get the point.)

### Jason & Kelli:

The "tools" you'll need for this mission of love is a blog or website, a picture, and a credit card. Intrigued?

If you don't already have one, get a blog and post a love letter, a poem and/or a collage of photos that show your love for your husband.

Instead of directly sending him the link to your blog entry or web page, he's going to "accidentally"

▶▶▶

**facebook** and Your Marriage

226

discover it through an Ad that sits in the sidebar on Facebook.

Once the blog or web post is live, go to your Facebook account and follow the prompts to "Create an Ad." Write out a headline that will catch his attention. Upload a photo (either of you or the two of you) into the ad that will ensure he won't miss it when it pops up. Type text into the ad that makes it obvious that he is the target of the ad. Once the ad looks the way you want it, geo-target it to make sure it shows up in your husband's rotation of ads.

Geo-targeting the FB Ad is easy. Target his gender (M), his marital status (Married), his geographic location (current town), and his age (give or take a couple of years). The more targeted the ad gets, the smaller the target audience number gets. That's a good thing because it betters the chance he'll discover the ad when he's on Facebook.

Now set up a date range of when the ad will run. Choose a three-day or longer period of time for the ad to better the chances that he'll see it sometime when he is on Facebook. The ad can be stopped at anytime, so if he sees it in the first hour that it runs, you can stop the ad from showing again.

The final part is to figure out how much you want to pay for each ad or for a number of impressions. More than likely, paying per click will make the most fiscal sense. Click rates can range from 30

cents to $2.00 per click depending on where you live and when you're running the ads. Since you are in a bidding war with other advertisers, a higher bid betters the chances that the ad runs more often. To ensure you don't go to the poorhouse with this idea, set a daily budget for the ad campaign that doesn't break the bank.

Once the ad is approved and begins to run, sit back and wait (and wait, and wait) for the ad to appear on the right side of his screen.

If it seems like nothing is happening, Facebook allows you to view the real-time results of the ad through the Ad Manager. You can view the impressions and clicks on your ad. Be patient. It may take a little time for the ad to make it into the right rotation at the right time.

### Jason:

And as a last resort, if you can't stand to wait any longer, you can show him the ad and expose the idea, the link, and the overall plan. It's not as fun and exciting, but at least he can appreciate the idea.

### Kelli:

Jason did this for me and I absolutely loved the fact that he plotted and planned so much to celebrate our 15th Anniversary.

**Jason:**

You can read about my experience of trying out this exact plan on my blog (MarriageJunkie.com — "How to Express 'Happy Anniversary' Using 21st Century Tools").

## Related Threads:

- ▶ **Sharing the Love Through Updates**............208
- ▶ **Go on Facebook Dates**........................214
- ▶ **Posting Poems & Love Posts**..................217
- ▶ **Special Moment Shout-Outs**...................222
- ▶ **Creative Invites to Date Your Mate**..........224

## Section 7

*What happens on Facebook does not stay on Facebook. And when married people do questionable things on Facebook, it can negatively impact their marriage. This thread series is intended to help spouses figure out how to handle a difficult situation when their Facebooking spouse has made poor choices and bad decisions on Facebook.*

- ▶ Spouse Spends Too Much Time on FB . . . . . . . . . . . . . . . 232
- ▶ Mate Is Chronic Updater. . . . . . . . . . . . . . . . . . . . . . . . . . . 235
- ▶ Having Insecurity Surges . . . . . . . . . . . . . . . . . . . . . . . . . . 238
- ▶ Concerns with Spouse Friending Exes . . . . . . . . . . . . . . . 242
- ▶ Spouse Broke Agreement on Friends . . . . . . . . . . . . . . . . 245
- ▶ Viewing Spouse's Chat Sessions . . . . . . . . . . . . . . . . . . . . 248
- ▶ Logging Into My Mate's Facebook . . . . . . . . . . . . . . . . . . . 251
- ▶ Is It an Emotional Affair? . . . . . . . . . . . . . . . . . . . . . . . . . . 254
- ▶ Caught Spouse but I'm to Blame? . . . . . . . . . . . . . . . . . . . 257
- ▶ Confronting Spouse About Affair. . . . . . . . . . . . . . . . . . . . 260
- ▶ Spouse Changes "Married" to "It's Complicated" . . . . 264
- ▶ Ex-Spouse OK as FB Friend?. . . . . . . . . . . . . . . . . . . . . . . 268
- ▶ Is Our Marriage Over?. . . . . . . . . . . . . . . . . . . . . . . . . . . . . 271
- ▶ Spouse Wants a Do-Over . . . . . . . . . . . . . . . . . . . . . . . . . . 274

230

# SOS! My Marriage Is Suffering Because of Facebook!

# Spouse Spends Too Much Time on FB

# SOS! My Marriage Is Suffering Because of Facebook!

## Numbers Don't Lie

Average user spends more than 55 minutes per day on Facebook.

My spouse is always on Facebook. She's on it from morning to night. She reads people's profiles, plays games, and takes quizzes all the time. I feel like the kids and I come second to Facebook. Any suggestions to help me pry my wife away from her computer?

### Jason & Kelli:

Facebook is a great way to spend small portions of the day, not for consuming an entire day. Unfortunately, Facebook can feed the insatiable appetite of busybodies, gossips, a bored spouse, or the lonely. And if people aren't careful, they can waste a lot of time online while neglecting their loved ones in real time.

### Kelli:

As wives and moms, we have so many demands on us by our families (and work) that we need our own way to veg out and regroup. Kids do this by texting or playing video games. Many husbands veg out watching TV. I know a number of moms who use Facebook to temporarily escape. It gives us that "adult" time we crave (especially if we're with the kids all day) and the relational booster shot we need. The risk is that we can overdose on our Facebook time just like kids can spend too much time texting and husbands can spend too much time in front of the TV.

▶▶▶

## facebook
### and Your Marriage

232

### Jason & Kelli:

So, for a spouse who seems to have lost sight of balancing their time and their most important relationships, a gentle confrontation needs to take place. Wait for a time when your wife is not on Facebook (and when the kids are preoccupied) to let her know you would like to set up a date to talk about your relationship and focus on making more time together and more time with the kids. We call this an "About Us" date.

### Jason:

She may be a little dazed and confused that her husband wants to talk about relationship stuff so you may have to repeat yourself.

### Jason & Kelli:

Whether the conversation takes place right then or later, keep in mind that Facebook itself is not the problem. The lack of time together is the problem with the core issues being that you crave more quality time with your wife and the kids want more time spent as a family.

Share with her how much you value her and that you want to find a way to spend more time together. Brainstorm some ways to carve out the time to become more intentional with your family time. Come up with ideas where all of you are

▶▶▶

spending less time in front of screens and more time with one another.

**Kelli:**

By everyone taking a step away from their screens and toward one another, this will likely give her the emotional and relational fix she needs to move her Facebook time more into balance.

**Jason & Kelli:**

If things don't change, then there may be a more serious issue. And if that's the case, you might want to bring in a third party (pastor, minister, rabbi, counselor or a therapist). On **FacebookAndYourMarriage.com**, we have links to different networks in case you don't have your own clergy or counselor.

## Related Threads:

- The "About Us" Date .........................334
- Calling for an "About Us" Date................338
- Setting Up Boundaries........................ 319
- Avoiding FB Addiction........................ 148
- Finding Solutions for Your FB Problems........328

# SOS! My Marriage Is Suffering Because of Facebook!

## Mate Is Chronic Updater

When we go out, my husband is on his phone updating his Facebook and reading other people's updates. This totally irritates me, but when I bring it up he blows me off. I don't look forward to our date nights because he spends so much time looking at his phone and not enough time looking at me. How do I get him to stop doing this?

### Jason & Kelli:

This is the blessing and curse of smart phones that have 365/24/7 Internet access. A person can access almost anything they want on the Internet at any time. But just because they can doesn't mean they should.

It sounds like you are really annoyed with your husband. To cool off a bit and help you focus your concerns, write down your thoughts and feelings and try to narrow your issues to one central issue. Are you feeling some rejection by your husband when he includes his network of friends in your date night? Are you sensing your sacred "us" time is being robbed and too many others are being included on your date? Are you more upset with his reaction to your bringing up the concern than the concern itself?

This little step will ultimately help you to communicate exactly what the problem is, which in turn makes resolving the problem less complicated.

### Did You Know?

Signs of imbalance with Facebook:

1. You lose sleep over Facebook
2. You spend more than an hour on Facebook
3. You become obsessed with old loves
4. You ignore work in favor of Facebook
5. Getting off Facebook leaves you in a cold sweat

▶▶▶

**facebook** and Your Marriage

### Jason:

Spouses often make the mistake of bringing up a grievance when they're in the moment and fuming hot. The thought is, if it's on our mind we want to make sure it is on our spouse's mind too. Try to find a time when you and your husband can talk without interruption (by the kids or a tight schedule where the conversation could be prematurely cut off). Or better yet, let him know you want to talk about a relationship issue and set up a time in the near future so you're both prepared to talk about it. We call this an "About Us" date.

### Jason & Kelli:

When it comes time for "the talk," ask him why he enjoys reading and posting FB updates so often. Whatever his answer, acknowledge and affirm that need. Let him know how much you value your time together and that you would like your date night to be as technology-free as possible.

Share with him your central issue when it comes to date nights, and suggest some boundaries for your date nights. Ideas like: checking Facebook during drive time only (for the non-driver only though), the phone is to be for phone calls only (and only from the babysitter or kids), no Facebook during main parts of date, no phone between the time of completing the meal and sexual intimacy that night. Choose a boundary or two and try it out to see if it works.

### Kelli:

It's common practice for movie theaters to ask people to turn off their phones because they distract both the user and others from the main reason they're in the room — to watch a movie. The same idea applies to date nights. Phones distract the user and their significant other from the main reason they're on the date night...to spend time with the one they love.

## Related Threads:

- ▶ The "About Us" Date . . . . . . . . . . . . . . . . . . . . . . . 334
- ▶ Go on Facebook Dates . . . . . . . . . . . . . . . . . . . . . 214
- ▶ Creating Your Own Boundaries . . . . . . . . . . . . . . 341
- ▶ Spouse Spends Too Much Time on FB . . . . . . . . 232
- ▶ The Right Amount of Updates . . . . . . . . . . . . . . . 88

# Having Insecurity Surges

### SOS! My Marriage Is Suffering Because of Facebook!

## Transform Your Relationship

**COUPLE COMMUNICATION**

Couple Communication is an award-winning program that helps you understand yourself and connect better as partners. Learn eleven skills and other processes to communicate effectively about day-to-day events and important issues.

**I'm normally a secure person, but ever since my husband and I have been on Facebook, I'm having insecurities as he reconnects with people from his years pre-me. We have a good marriage, but I can't shake these feelings. Help!**

### Jason & Kelli:

It's not uncommon for couples to experience some unfamiliar feelings when one's spouse is on Facebook, especially when they're just getting started. Each of you comes face to face with many from your prior life, and through the reminiscing and replaying of the past, one spouse is stuck on the virtual sidelines. They don't know the people, the references, or the situations. Perhaps for the first time in the marriage, a spouse is feeling like the odd man (or woman) out.

Reconnecting with people via Facebook can stir up a lot of emotions and feelings, baggage and past hurts, and issues that go back to high school, junior high, or earlier. Some get swept up by their emotions, and others simply block out those past experiences and the drama that went with them. And if you're wading through a flurry of remembrances that spark old feelings and memories, your spouse is probably experiencing the same thing. And that's where the uncomfortable feelings can stem from. While you have a lot of power controlling your own

▶▶▶

**facebook** *and Your Marriage*

feelings, you're virtually powerless to help your spouse control theirs...unless you talk about it.

**Kelli:**

So what's your problem? Really, you need to figure out what your concerns are before you can expect your husband to do anything about it.

**Jason:**

Ever since Kelli and I started on Facebook, we've made it a habit of sharing with each other who we've become FB Friends with or gotten Friend Requests from. It always makes for an interesting conversation sharing about so-and-so and how we know them. So, when Kelli told me she had just become FB Friends with an old boyfriend, my facial expression showed genuine interest, but my mind began thinking.

After her brief update about him, my mind kept thinking. After a few exchanged Wall postings and comments, my mind kept thinking. The time came to share with her how I felt, but I didn't exactly know what I was feeling. After 14 years of marriage, jealousy was new terrain for me.

### Jason & Kelli:

Take some time to explore your feelings. Are you feeling jealous, worried, anxious, or all of the above? Has your husband done something to stoke these feelings? Is there something that happened in your past (or his) that makes these reconnections seem like a potential threat to your relationship?

Once you have a handle on your feelings and what may be triggering them, sit down with your husband and share them. Ask if he has experienced any feelings on his end (either with his own Facebook experience or yours). Give each other some time and space to explore your feelings and talk about them honestly.

### Jason:

After some time of thinking, praying, and journaling, I had a pretty good grip on my feelings and my issues. I was able to share with Kelli my concerns which kicked off a series of "About Us" dates. Over time, we both processed what was and was not going on and create some new guard rails for who we do and do not accept as FB Friends.

**Kelli:**

Being on a social network and reconnecting with people from our past was all new to us. There are a flood of emotions and memories that spark with each new FB Friend. Over several weeks, we talked a lot about our feelings and our concerns. It was out of those conversations that we were able to set up some boundaries for our relationships on Facebook.

**Jason & Kelli:**

If you want the insecurity feelings to go away, you need to address the issue with your husband. Time alone won't make the feelings go away. Time after talking with him and setting boundaries in place will.

## Related Threads:

- ▶ The "About Us" Date . . . . . . . . . . . . . . . . . . . . . . . . 334
- ▶ Should Married Facebookers Beware? . . . . . . . . . . 60
- ▶ Concerns with Spouse Friending Exes . . . . . . . . . 282
- ▶ Friend Requests from Old Flames . . . . . . . . . . . . . 179
- ▶ Talking Without Fighting . . . . . . . . . . . . . . . . . . . . 314

# Concerns With Spouse Friending Exes

## Our Book Club Picks

*Not "Just" Friends* by Shirley Glass explains how infidelity- any secret sexual, romantic, or emotional involvement -violates commitment to an exclusive relationship and helps readers protect their relationship from infidelity and heal from the trauma of betrayal.

**I just found out that my wife has become FB Friends with some old boyfriends, but I'm uncomfortable with this. How do I share my concern without looking like a jealous husband?**

### Jason & Kelli:

This is a must-have conversation for married couples where one or both of them are on Facebook. And the earlier, the better.

This can also be one of the hardest conversations for a Facebooking couple to kick off. You don't want to presume something inappropriate is happening, you don't want to sound like you're overly possessive and suspicious, and you don't want to come across as an insecure and non-trusting spouse.

### Jason:

Let's move this scenario into a real-life parallel. If you and your wife went to a party and you saw her talk with another guy, what would you think? (Probably nothing.) If you saw her go into another room and close the door behind her, what would you think? (Probably nothing.) If you saw her go into a room with another guy, an ex-boyfriend, and he closed the door behind them, what would you think? (Now the thoughts are spinning, heart is pumping, and feet are moving.) While nothing

▶▶▶

may be happening, the scenario doesn't look or feel right, and therefore it isn't right. Whether the motivation is insecurity, jealous tendencies, or sensing a threat, anyone who is married has the responsibility to proactively protect their spouse, their marriage, and their family.

### Jason & Kelli:

Before you talk with her, take some time to think through your concerns, how you're going to express them, and ideas for joint boundaries that the two of you can agree on.

Are your concerns fueled by past experiences, news stories of rekindled romances via Facebook, or a yearning for healthy boundaries to be set? Maybe a combination of the three.

When you share your concerns, give her time to process them. Encourage her to think through why she would want to reunite and be in regular contact with an old boyfriend through Facebook. She may embrace your concerns, or she may be defensive toward them.

### Kelli:

I was a little defensive with Jason when he brought up a similar concern. I was happy in my marriage and not thinking of doing anything inappropriate by being FB Friends with an old boyfriend. At first

I thought Jason was insinuating that something was going on. But as I heard his concerns and thought through it more, I didn't know what was going on in the old boyfriend's mind or how his wife felt about her husband reconnecting with an old girlfriend. Most importantly, I knew what my husband thought and how he felt about it. I Unfriended the old boyfriend.

**Jason & Kelli:**

About six or so months into being on Facebook, we made the decision (together) that we would not be FB Friends with anyone we had any sort of an intimate past with. We each went through and Unfriended people from our past and have since declined Friend Requests from others. This new boundary is something we agreed made sense for us. What are boundaries that the two of you need to set with your time on Facebook?

### Related Threads:

- ▸ Friend Requests from Old Flames . . . . . . . . . . . . . 179
- ▸ Declining Friend Requests with Dignity . . . . . . . . .118
- ▸ Hiding, Removing & Blocking People . . . . . . . . . .191
- ▸ Finding Solutions for Your FB Problems. . . . . . . .328
- ▸ Setting Up Boundaries . . . . . . . . . . . . . . . . . . . . . . 319

# SOS! My Marriage Is Suffering Because of Facebook!

## Spouse Broke Agreement on Friends

**When we started on Facebook, my husband and I agreed that we wouldn't become FB Friends with old flames. I've stuck with my end of the bargain, but my husband hasn't. He's become FB Friends with two old girlfriends and an ex-fiancee. He has commented on their photos and written on their Walls. I went ballistic on him, and rather than manning up he says that I'm overreacting on a non-issue. Excuse me? What should I do?**

### Jason & Kelli:

Anytime an agreed upon boundary line gets crossed, the betrayed and the betrayer react in a couple of predictable ways.

The natural response of the betrayed one is to take the hurt feelings, mix it with some righteous indignation, add a little rage and let loose with a sharply worded confrontation toward the betrayer.

When this happens, the betrayer will have one of three responses of his own: one is to blow up and retaliate; another is to minimize the betrayal; and the last possible response is to run away from the confrontation. All of these are different ways for the betrayer to protect himself from the guilt he is feeling.

---

### Our Book Club Picks

*Soul Healing Love* is a reader-friendly book, with theoretical and spiritual integrity that exudes hope for couples. With so many books about how to fix a marriage, this one stands out and gets rave reviews. That's because it offers an optimistic, joyful approach based on easy-to-understand, easy-to-apply, practical steps for creating the soul-mate marriages we all dream about.

▶▶▶

## facebook
### and Your Marriage

Unfortunately, none of the reactions (by the betrayer or the betrayed) works very well to resolve any kind of issue.

So, let's move toward a plan that can work. Collect your thoughts, reflect on your feelings, and then choose your words wisely. Ask your husband for an "About Us" date to help you sort through the changes to your agreed upon policy about friending exes and for you two to reevaluate the boundaries that were originally set up and reestablish a new one you both can live with.

This is an opportunity for you to turn toward each other instead of away from one another. You'll be able to discuss any confusion and hurt feelings surrounding the original boundaries, and set up new boundaries you both can live with.

### Jason:

And the new boundaries may end up being the old boundaries you originally set up, but now with a greater understanding and appreciation for why you made them in the first place.

### Kelli:

It's important that there's full transparency as you talk with each other. Here's some questions for you to consider: What was our intent in establishing the original boundary? Why do you want to reestablish relationships with past love interests? What are you hoping to accomplish with these reestablished connections? How will they improve our marriage? If we are to remove the previously agreed on boundary line, what would the new boundary line be? What happens if one of us wants to ignore that boundary line?

### Jason & Kelli:

It may be a good idea to bring in a neutral third party (counselor, clergy, mentor couple, relationship coach) to provide accountability and ensure civility with your discussion. There's a pretty good list of networks to tap into at **FacebookAndYourMarriage.com**. Ultimately, new boundaries (stronger and firmer than the previous) must be set up, agreed upon, and followed.

## Related Threads:

- Friending Exes...or Not?...................164
- Calling for an "About Us" Date.............338
- Creating Your Own Boundaries..............341
- Living Inbounds...........................344
- Finding Help..............................349

# Viewing Spouse's Chat Sessions

## Our Book Club Picks

*Staying Together* by Stephen Judah explores the phenomenon of infidelity, considering both the push of marital discord and the pull of sexual temptation. With clear and helpful analysis of the relational science behind infidelity, readers learn a tested way back toward a meaningful marriage.

**I have a suspicion that my wife is chatting with an old boyfriend she found on Facebook. Is there a way to see a record of her Chat sessions?**

### Jason & Kelli:

You're not going to like this answer, all Chat sessions are erased upon logging out of Facebook.

But you know what? The fastest way to alleviate your suspicions (and all the mental games you're playing on yourself) is to talk with your wife.

### Jason:

But don't set up the conversation with attitude or lead off with the accusation. This is a sure-fire way to tick her off, create more tension, and NOT get the answers you're looking for.

### Jason & Kelli:

When it's just the two of you (with little or no interruptions in sight), start a conversation about your Facebook experiences. Ask and answer questions such as: Who do you connect with on Facebook? Do you get much email from people on Facebook? Who from? Do you use the Chat feature? How often do you chat and with whom?

▶▶▶

**facebook** and Your Marriage

This will set up a more informed discussion on boundaries, protect your marriage from possible threats, and creat agreed upon rules for both of you on Facebook. This provides an appropriate and non-confrontational backdrop for asking your wife about your concern. Let her know your feelings about having private communications with past love interests.

**Kelli:**

And not just for her, but for you as well. And maybe you need to go one step further and not be FB Friends with past boyfriends/girlfriends.

**Jason & Kelli:**

With active communication, established boundaries, and regular conversations about your Facebook activities, give her an opportunity to live by your new agreed upon rules.

If after some time there is still reason for concern, have a more direct and pointed conversation about the boundary line that you feel may have been crossed. Hopefully, resolution and restoration can occur at that point.

If after another conversation you are convinced that she is lying, there is a final step you can take to either confirm your suspicions or validate your wife's assertions.

**Jason:**

But this is only if you are absolutely convinced that a major indiscretion is taking place.

**Jason & Kelli:**

There are screen shot software packages that take "photos" of the screen every few seconds and keep a log of those screens. This is a last resort option you could take.

**Kelli:**

This should not be used to snoop or spy on your spouse's time on Facebook or the Internet. It is a last resort if all other steps to find answers have been tried and failed.

## Related Threads:

- About the Chat Feature . . . . . . . . . . . . . . . . . . . . . . . 96
- Chatting Boundaries . . . . . . . . . . . . . . . . . . . . . . . . 162
- Friending Exes...or Not? . . . . . . . . . . . . . . . . . . . . . 164
- Talking Without Fighting . . . . . . . . . . . . . . . . . . . . 314
- Calling for an "About Us" Date . . . . . . . . . . . . . . . 338

# SOS! My Marriage Is Suffering Because of Facebook!

## Logging into My Mate's Facebook

I have a strong feeling my husband is emailing a woman he met on FB. I know his ID and password. Is it OK if I log on and check it? I'm hoping that I am wrong, but I sense that something is not right.

### Jason & Kelli:

In any situation where a spouse has suspicions about their mate's faithfulness, the best first step is always to have a conversation.

A conversation is not a diatribe, a debate, or an accusation-filled confrontation. It is giving your spouse the benefit of the doubt by providing him or her with an opportunity to respond to your concerns.

While we believe that having each other's log in information is a sign of mutual respect and trust, using it on a whim or to secretly rummage through a Facebook account searching for suspicious activity can breed the opposite of mutual respect and trust.

Spend some time sorting through your feelings and thoughts so when the time comes to express your concerns, you can do so rationally and calmly. By setting up an "About Us" date, your husband won't feel completely blindsided on the issue.

### Our Book Club Picks

*The Divorce Remedy* by Michele Weiner-Davis is an empowering and encouraging guide for revitalizing marriage and building stronger, more loving bonds. Learn how to manage marital problems and get your marriage back on track.

## facebook and Your Marriage

**Kelli:**

Remember to give him the benefit of the doubt.

**Jason:**

And the issue may not be completely resolved in one sitting.

**Jason & Kelli:**

After your discussion, if there is still doubt or suspicion, ask your husband if you could view his FB Inbox. If he rejects your request, it would seem you have justifiable grounds to log in and view his account (at a later time).

But if you take this course of action, be ready for your next step of responsibility. If you find evidence that confirms your suspicions, you'll need to seek some help for yourself and help for your marriage.

Or, if there is no evidence to support your suspicions, you will owe your husband an acknowledgement of your actions and an apology, and you will need to ask for his forgiveness.

**Kelli:**

And it's probably still a good idea to get some counseling or attend a marriage education program. We have links to all kinds of programs at **FacebookAndYourMarriage.com**.

## Related Threads:

- **Password Exchange** . . . . . . . . . . . . . . . . . . . . . . . . . . 146
- **Facebook Email** . . . . . . . . . . . . . . . . . . . . . . . . . . . . . . . 94
- **Spouse Overreacting on Friend Choices** . . . . . . . 284
- **Setting Up Boundaries** . . . . . . . . . . . . . . . . . . . . . . . 319
- **The "About Us" Date** . . . . . . . . . . . . . . . . . . . . . . . . 334

## Transform Your Relationship

**Weekend to Remember** offers couples a get-away with a purpose to rediscover each other and find more intimacy in your life together.

I can't shake this feeling! I think my husband is on his way to having an affair with someone on Facebook. Is that weird to think? Most of his FB Friends are women, and many of them are women I don't know. They post stuff on his Wall and comment on his Status Updates a lot, and he does the same. Am I being paranoid or is there a real concern here? I would love any feedback you could provide because my gut is telling me something is up.

### Jason & Kelli:

When our gut feelings start sending us signals, it is a great time to hit the pause button and give the mind some time to add some logic and thought to what the gut is saying.

Adultery and infidelity expert Dave Carder writes, "(M)any times when men and women who have had affairs are telling their story, they begin by saying, 'It all started so innocently....'"

### Jason:

BTW, Carder is an expert in the field because he's written several books on the topic. Not because he has vast personal experience in having affairs. Just saying...

### Jason & Kelli:

In *Close Calls*, Carder lays out four phases of an affair (or a "close call" to an affair). The first phase is *Growing Mutual Attraction*, when a spouse has an emotional and/or physical attraction to someone else. The second phase is *Entanglement*, which is where infatuation gives way to fantasy, a sharing of feelings occurs, and emotional intensity grows between the parties — and at some point erotic activity takes place. The third phase is *Destabilization of the Relationship* when the partners are conflicted with concern for one another but try to stop the relationship, often coming with physical or emotional consequences. The fourth phase is *Termination and Resolution* when the affair either breaks up the marriage or the marriage breaks up the affair.

When people join Facebook and (a) don't set boundaries of who they will and will not accept as FB Friends, (b) don't set guard rails for their interactions with people of the opposite sex, and (c) are ignorant of how emotional and physical affairs get started, they can find themselves well into the Emotional and Sexual Entanglement phase before they realize what's going on. And then a range of feelings kick in that skew reality and justify irresponsibility.

Sort through your own feelings and issues first, and then ask your husband for an "About Us" date. Ask him what need(s) is getting met through his female FB Friends and exchanges. Share with him how you feel about the higher than normal level of exchanges and some of your newfound wisdom on the phases of an affair. Be sure to listen to him as he talks (try to put yourself in his shoes) and try to identify some of the unmet needs that he may have.

Be ready for one, two, or three next steps: (1) both of you setting up some new boundaries for your Facebook experience; (2) both of you attending a marriage enrichment or marriage education communication program; (3) either solo or as a couple, find a marriage or sex therapist to help rebuild intimacy and trust between you.

**Kelli:**

If you don't know where to turn on number 2 or 3, check out **FacebookAndYourMarriage.com** for a list of local, regional and national resources.

### Related Threads:

- Hiding, Removing & Blocking People . . . . . . . . . . . 191
- Confronting Spouse About Affair . . . . . . . . . . . . 260
- Calling for an "About Us" Date . . . . . . . . . . . . . . . 338
- Working Through Infidelity Together . . . . . . . . . 346
- Finding Help . . . . . . . . . . . . . . . . . . . . . . . . . . . . . . . 349

# SOS! My Marriage Is Suffering Because of Facebook!

## Caught Spouse but I'm to Blame?

**I walked into our home office the other day and glanced at the computer screen and noticed that my wife's Facebook was still logged in and on the screen (she had gone to the bathroom). The Chat box was still up and I read some of the Chat exchanges she was having with a guy. They were really flirty, borderline sexual. She walked in and when I asked her about the messages, she got upset that I had read her "private" chats. She said she was just playing around and that she didn't mean it. Should I be concerned here?**

### Jason & Kelli:

Absolutely, positively, without reservation, bolded, in all caps, and underlined seven times...YES!

Now that you know your concerns are valid (you wouldn't have written the question if you weren't concerned) you're probably wondering how to broach the topic with her.

Arrange an "About Us" date with your wife. When you are together, replay the scenario as you explained it to us and ask her, "Help me understand, if it is OK to flirt with other people in private Chat sessions, why did you get so defensive about it when I discovered it?"

Be ready for all kinds of responses to this question.

▶▶▶

## facebook
### and Your Marriage

If she continuously defends the actions or deflects the issue back onto you for viewing the message (by trying to make you feel guilty for reading her "private" chats) share with her your feelings about her seeking that kind of attention from another man.

Restate your commitment to her and your marriage, and that you would not engage in a racy or flirty Chat session (or live conversation) with another woman.

If she has a change of heart, then the two of you need to talk about setting up mutually beneficial and agreed upon boundaries for your Facebook (and other online) time, and possibly establish some individual accountability with close friends, a pastor, or a counselor.

**Kelli:**

It would probably be a good idea for both of you to turn off the Chat feature for a period of time while you're working on your relationship.

**Jason:**

Or turn it off indefinitely.

**Jason & Kelli:**

If there is no change of heart after your first "About Us" date, give it a day or two. Hopefully she'll realize her actions were out of bounds and admit her fault in the matter.

If the "About Us" date doesn't go well or if she's not willing to acknowledge that the Chat exchange was wrong, you should seek professional help from a clergy, a counselor or both.

## Related Threads:

- About the Chat Feature . . . . . . . . . . . . . . . . . . . . . . . 96
- Is It an Emotional Affair? . . . . . . . . . . . . . . . . . . . . . 254
- The "About Us" Date . . . . . . . . . . . . . . . . . . . . . . . 334
- Hiding, Removing & Blocking People . . . . . . . . . . 191
- Finding Help . . . . . . . . . . . . . . . . . . . . . . . . . . . . . . 349

# Confronting Spouse About Affair

## Our Book Club Picks

*Infidelity* by Dr. Don-David Lusterman takes what he has learned in thousands of hours of counseling clients how to cope with infidelity, and shares a step-by-step approach to deal with the emotional impact of the affair and where to go from there.

---

I just discovered my spouse has been emailing an ex-boyfriend on Facebook for months, and they have even met up for coffee. She never told me this. I found out by reading an email in her FB Inbox. I am furious, hurt, confused, and can't get out of my head that she might be having an affair. How do I confront her about this without losing it?

### Jason & Kelli:

First, breathe. Take several deep breaths. Your wife has betrayed your trust, but at this point all you know is that she met with this guy. It may have been to tell him how much she loves you. It may be an action step she now regrets. But before you jump to too many conclusions, get your head right.

Find someone you trust and talk with them about what you discovered, how you're feeling, and what's racing around in your head. Your friend, your pastor, your therapist — they should be able to help you think this through and diffuse some of the built up energy you've got.

### Jason:

Journaling is a fantastic way to safely vent and help you figure out what you're feeling. Set the pen down to paper or go crazy tapping on the keyboard and get your words out...all of them!

▶▶▶

**facebook** and Your Marriage

260

# SOS! My Marriage Is Suffering Because of Facebook!

## Confronting Spouse About Affair

In a short period of time, you'll have captured your thoughts and feelings. Journaling helps you figure out what to say and how to say it. It can also help you figure out what not to say. This greatly reduces the chances of saying something stupid or something you will later regret.

### Jason & Kelli:

Once you've got a handle on what needs to be said, set up an "About Us" date with your wife.

When the "About Us" date occurs, don't start the conversation by making accusations, assertions, or indictments. Simply explain what you discovered, how you feel about it, and let her know you don't understand it. Invite her to explain it. She won't know how long you've been stewing on this, what you've done to cool down, and the steps you've taken to prepare for this moment, so give her some time to process what she's heard.

### Kelli:

So don't take what is said at the moment as gospel truth. She may need some time to think about what she's done, why she's done it, the pain it has caused, and where to go from here.

▶▶▶

**facebook** and Your Marriage

### Jason & Kelli:

The key to moving forward lies in a few questions. How do you make your relationship stronger? What steps need to be taken to rebuild trust and commitment in your marriage? What will you do to ensure this kind of situation does not happen again?

These are questions only the two of you can answer. And those answers will need to be something you both can live with and live up to.

### Kelli:

In the midst of your discussion, give each other permission to be human — with your emotions, your words, your reactions. No one is perfect and sometimes we can find ourselves in a much different place than we ever imagined, and having to admit fault for something we never dreamed could occur. When that happens, the right answers don't always come out the first time.

### Jason & Kelli:

Forgiveness is essential in marriage. While we never know when we need to expend it, our marriage will benefit from it when we do.

**Jason:**

And if you find yourself in a position where you're constantly doling out forgiveness and she is promising "It will never happen again," you'll need to set up some more boundaries so you're not being taken advantage of. A counselor, a clergy, or a good friend can help you with this.

**Jason & Kelli:**

Forgiveness won't instantly improve the quality of your relationship. But it can keep the two of you and your relationship on the pathway to healing, improvement, and eventually, greatness.

## Related Threads:

- Friending Exes...or Not?...................164
- Hiding, Removing & Blocking People..........191
- Is It an Emotional Affair?.....................254
- The "About Us" Date......................334
- Finding Solutions for Your FB Problems........328

# Spouse Changes "Married" to "It's Complicated"

## Making a Difference

**WinShape Marriage**

WinShape Retreat hosts marriage intensives conducted by a partnership of several other organizations to provide intensive small-group sessions to find lasting solutions to serious marital struggles by exposing the root of the problem. Emotional connections are reestablished and couples recover safety in their relationship with each other, leading to true intimacy and genuine healing.

---

**My wife and I are going through some tough times and have just separated. She just changed her Relationship Status to "it's complicated." This just kills me! I think we can work it through, but this step makes our private issues public. What can I say to her to change her status back to married?**

### Jason & Kelli:

Sorry to hear about the tough season you and your wife are in.

Before you talk with her, try to figure out why it bothers you so much. Are you embarrassed that others now know you're having some problems? Are you fearful she is giving up on the marriage?

Also, think about why she would change her Relationship Status. Is she calling out for help? Is she trying to get attention from others? Or, is she trying to get your attention?

### Jason:

Many couples who have a "plan" for their separation end up reuniting and with some hard work have a stronger relationship than before the separation. These "plans" revolve around couples rebuilding the foundation for their relationship and acquiring new relationship skills. Separation plans can include counseling, marriage intensives,

▶▶▶

**facebook** and Your Marriage

264

attending marriage retreats, and participating in marriage education programs (we have a bunch listed on **FacebookAndYourMarriage.com**.) Also, planned separations include a set timeline so couples can objectively measure their goals and progress toward reconciliation.

### Jason & Kelli:

Do you and your wife have a planned separation? Most couples don't attach a plan to their separation. If not, what is your plan to move your relationship from "it's complicated" to "married"? What practical steps to improve the relationship does your wife need to hear from you in order to replace her doubt and confusion with hope and confidence?

When you have answers to why the Relationship Status change bothers you, why you think your wife may have made the change, and most importantly tangible plans to reconcile your relationship, then you're ready to talk with her.

Assuming there are no legal reasons preventing you from contacting her, call her and let her know you have been thinking a lot about your relationship. Invite her to meet with you for a time to talk.

### Kelli:

We call this an "About Us" date and encourage you to follow the steps for the "About Us" date but because of the delicacy of your situation, don't *call* it an "About Us" date.

### Jason & Kelli:

If and when you meet with her, be prepared with what you're going to say. And be even more prepared not to get overly emotional and react to what she says. You have spent time thinking and processing and perhaps she hasn't. When you do meet up, start the conversation by trying to understand her and her concerns before jumping into your own concerns.

Let her know you're committed to the marriage and what steps you will take to fight for your marriage. Ask her what she'll do to work on the relationship. Ask her if there is something more you could do on your part for the relationship. Then let her know how changing her Relationship Status to "It's Complicated" affects you. Request that she change it back to "married." If she doesn't want to make the change, it's not the end of the world. You have made a commitment to her and set up a plan to reconcile. With some hard work, some real change and some time, there will likely be a point she will change it back to "married"... and mean it.

**SOS! My Marriage Is Suffering Because of Facebook!**     Spouse Changes "Married" to "It's Complicated"

**Kelli:**

There are all kinds of great support systems, helpful books and amazing resources we have at **FacebookAndYourMarriage.com** to help you be successful in making the changes you're determined to make.

## Related Threads:

- ▶ Let Facebook Know You're Married............150
- ▶ Changing My Status to "It's Complicated"......288
- ▶ Talking Without Fighting.....................314
- ▶ The "About Us" Date ........................334
- ▶ Finding Help...............................349

**facebook** and Your Marriage

## Making a Difference

Marriage Works! Ohio is a collaborative effort to help build healthy families and healthy communities by providing marriage and relationship education for couples.

Marriage Works! Ohio offers a variety of classes and workshops for couples at every stage in their relationships, whether dating, living together, considering marriage, or married.

---

**Is there a reason my husband should be FB Friends with his ex-wife? They didn't have kids, so in my opinion there is no reason to keep in contact. They have been divorced for seven years (we've been married for three years and have a one-year-old son.) He believes it's not that big of a deal. I believe differently. She has posted some posts that are over the line. Help!**

### Jason & Kelli:

If there are no kids or no joint business ventures, then no, there is no reason for him to keep in contact with her, especially on Facebook. What do you mean "over the line"?

### Questioner:

On what would have been their 15th wedding anniversary, she wrote, "If we were still together it would have been 15 years today." And she tagged him in some photos from when they were married in an album titled "Old photos."

### Jason & Kelli:

OK, she has clearly crossed over the line. Your husband needs to take a firm stand with her that includes Facebook's version of banishment, by Blocking her. But before he does, he needs to

▶▶▶

contact her and request that any photos from their married days not be posted on Facebook.

### Kelli:

If she tagged him in the pictures, he can at least untag his name from the photos.

### Jason & Kelli:

He should also let her know that he will be Blocking her because her actions are inappropriate, out of bounds, and rude to his current wife and family.

Your husband is either minimizing the incidents to either avoid confrontation or downplaying the seriousness of the situation out of ignorance. You need to initiate the steps to resolve the issue by asking him for an "About Us" date.

So when you do talk with him, start it off by asking him why he wants to remain in contact with his ex-wife. Then invite him to view the scenario by standing in your shoes and ask him how he thinks this affects you. Restate his reasons and then share your feelings toward him and his actions due to his staying in contact with his ex-wife. Explain how it affects you and how it could affect your friends and family. Suggest that boundaries be set up immediately to protect himself, you, and your children from his ex-wife. Then show him how easy it is to Block someone

▶▶▶

on Facebook (find step-by-step instructions at **FacebookAndYourMarriage.com**).

If at the end of your conversation he is still pooh-poohing the matter, suggest he get input from a few of your pre-screened friends or talk to a trusted third party.

**Jason:**

If he's still not connecting the dots here, have him read this: Dude! Man up and protect your wife and your family from your ex-wife. Whether the ex's actions were fueled by malice for your wife, desire for you, or complete ignorance, step up and make the right choice NOW! Block this woman and don't look back! As a husband, your biggest priority in life is to go all out in your love for your wife! Your ex-wife doesn't fit into that equation.

## Related Threads:

- ▶ Friending Exes...or Not?.......................164
- ▶ Turning Screaming Matches into Conversations..325
- ▶ Calling for an "About Us" Date................338
- ▶ Hiding, Removing & Blocking People..........191
- ▶ Spouse Overreacting on Friend Choices.......284

SOS! My Marriage Is Suffering Because of Facebook! — IS OUR MARRIAGE OVER?

**My husband is having an affair! He reconnected with his former girlfriend on Facebook and now he's telling me that he's found his "soul mate." My 12-year marriage has been stolen and I am completely heartbroken! Is there something I can do to win him back?**

### Jason & Kelli:

We are so very sorry to hear this news.

### Kelli:

But the good news is that while it takes just one spouse to ruin a marriage, it can also take just one spouse to rescue a marriage.

### Jason & Kelli:

There is nothing you can do to force change or make change happen. But you can let him know you are standing for the marriage and invite him back into the marriage.

There are a number of good books, websites, and support groups that have helped betrayed spouses walk this courageous path. (We're constantly updating the list of resources at **FacebookAndYourMarriage.com**.) Check them out and see what works for you.

## Our Book Club Picks

*Shattered Vows* offers hope and healing in this sensitive and practical guide with proven tools that help women struggling with sexual betrayal. Inspired by the author's personal journey through betrayal, her extensive work with hurting women, and her intimate marriage two decades after her husband's infidelity.

**facebook** and Your Marriage

## Our Book Club Picks

*Divorce Busting* by Michele Weiner-Davis gives straightforward, effective advice on how couples can stay together instead of coming apart. Her marriage-enriching, divorce-preventing techniques are good enough to help even just one spouse save a marriage.

Next, find someone you can talk with (a therapist, a pastor, a good friend) who will help you talk through your own pain, feelings, and issues.

### Kelli:

Create a support system of people who can be your source of strength, hope, and encouragement during this dark season. Find friends and family who you can trust. As tempting as it may be, this is not a time to push people away. It is a time to find people to pull into your world and allow them to emotionally support you. If you don't have these people in your life, find a church in your area.

### Jason:

And for ethical, social and legal reasons, don't give specifics about what is happening in your marriage on Facebook. Keep the specifics of your situation for your real-time support system. Oh, and don't change your Relationship Status either.

### Jason & Kelli:

As you work on you, set up firm boundaries for your sake and the kids (if you have any) and your walk-away spouse. This keeps a healthy distance between his drama and your sanity.

▶▶▶

You also need to identify the line between standing for your marriage on one side and protecting yourself legally on the other. Especially if your husband's infidelity persists, his defiance toward the marriage continues, and his rejection of the marriage vows remains.

In her book *The Divorce Remedy*, Michelle Weiner-Davis offers this advice to spouses standing for their marriage when the other spouse is actively having an affair: "This is not the optimum situation as you can well imagine but it's not time to give up hope just yet. For one thing...most affairs end within six months. Second, affairs usually don't result in marriage, and when they do, most end in divorce. So if you're desperate to save your marriage, and you have enough patience to wait this thing out, you may just be able to turn things around."

This is the best advice to get, and the hardest advice to follow. Take it one day at a time.

## Related Threads:

- ▶ Friending Exes...or Not?....................164
- ▶ Leaving My Marriage ......................304
- ▶ Spouse Wants a Do-Over...................274
- ▶ Working Through Infidelity Together.........346
- ▶ Finding Help...............................349

# Spouse Wants a Do-Over

## SOS! My Marriage Is Suffering Because of Facebook!

### Our Book Club Picks

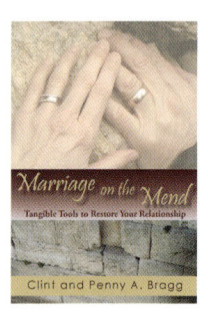

*Marriage on the Mend* equips readers with innovative and tangible tools that were developed during the first five years of the authors' own marital reconciliation, following an eleven-year divorce. Couples choosing to reconcile after repeated marital conflicts, separation, or even divorce face a unique set of challenges. This book gives couples hope and a plan.

---

**My wife has asked me to forgive her for a short affair she was having with someone she met on Facebook. I thought we had the perfect marriage and then this happened. What do I do?**

### Jason & Kelli:

We've read that "the revelation of an infidelity is most shocking and horrifying in those marriages that had seemed 'perfect.'"

Many couples have traveled the path of recovery and ascended from that low and dark place to the highlands where their marriage is transformed and becomes healthy, vitally strong and intimate.

Having said that, you'll need counsel for this journey (a marriage therapist, a pastor, or one who specializes in infidelity recovery.) They can keep you accountable and help ensure you both continue doing your part to make the relationship whole again. You can find some helpful resources at **FacebookAndYourMarriage.com**.

As with all journeys, they take time and energy. Both of you will need time and energy to sort through your individual feelings, to discuss how this happened, and to talk about what needs to change to make sure it doesn't happen again.

Sometimes journeys can take us to unexpected places that deliver unanticipated results. To subdue those crazy thoughts and images in your

▶▶▶

**facebook** and Your Marriage

274

mind, it may be helpful to have an "About Us" date where you're able to ask about the specifics of her affair.

This is a onetime offer with the agreement that after she honestly answers your questions, the specifics of the affair cannot be discussed, rehashed or replayed again.

The journey to rebuild trust, commitment, and intimacy in a marriage is tough. Thankfully you are not alone, and there are all kinds of resources to help you and your wife overcome the betrayal and make your marriage strong and healthy once again.

### Jason:

A therapist friend of mine shared that healing from an affair is much like healing from a bad cut. It's tender for a while, but over time the scar tissue heals stronger than the normal tissue.

### Kelli:

And over time, even though the scar is still there, you remember that it is there less and less.

**Jason:**

Find people who love you and your wife and want to see your marriage survive the infidelity. You will need their support and encouragement on this journey.

### Related Threads:

- ▶ Setting Up Boundaries..................319
- ▶ Hiding, Removing & Blocking People..........191
- ▶ Repairing a Marriage I Messed Up............308
- ▶ Working Through Infidelity Together.........346
- ▶ Finding Help................................349

## Section 8

*Reconnecting with people from one's past can be a fun and thrilling experience. Problem? Some reconnections are not good for one's marriage. This thread is intended to help Facebookers sort through their feelings and emotions as well as their choices and actions before, during or after making marriage-threatening decisions.*

- ▶ Make Past Boy/Girlfriend a Current FB Friend?........280
- ▶ Ex's Profile Pic Sparks Feelings......................282
- ▶ Spouse Overreacting on Friend Choices...............284
- ▶ Can't Wait to Facebook with Someone................286
- ▶ Changing My Status to "It's Complicated"............288
- ▶ My Spouse Is Spying on Me..........................291
- ▶ Rekindled Romance on Facebook.....................294
- ▶ From Facebook to Face-to-Face......................298
- ▶ Am I About to Have an Affair?.......................301
- ▶ Leaving My Marriage................................304
- ▶ Repairing a Marriage I Messed Up...................308

# Seriously? Let's Think This Through a Bit More

# Make Past Boy/Girlfriend a Current FB Friend?

**Seriously? Let's Think This Through a Bit More**

## Making a Difference

**The National Healthy Marriage Resource Center (NHMRC)** is a clearinghouse for high quality, balanced, and timely information and resources on healthy marriage. NHMRC provides resources and training for experts, researchers, policymakers, media, marriage educators, couples and individuals, and program providers.

**I just found an old boyfriend on Facebook. Should I send him a Friend Request? Should I tell my husband if my old beau accepts the request?**

### Jason & Kelli:

It's natural to wonder what happened to people of the past. But when it comes to past dating interests, crushes, steady partners, and one-night stands, pause before you accept or initiate the Friend Request. The same curiosity that killed the cat can also kill (or threaten) your marriage.

Think we're being a little extreme?

What feelings did you experience when you typed his name into the Search box? Or saw his name and Profile Picture? Or saw the Friend Suggestion? Be honest.

Those feelings are fueled by the past with no sense of the present and no concern for your future.

This is where commitment to your marriage, respect for your husband, and consideration for healthy boundaries need to kick in.

### Jason:

Saying "I do" to your spouse on the wedding day was saying "I don't" to anyone who poses a potential threat to your marriage covenant. In my

**facebook** *and Your Marriage*

# Seriously? Let's Think This Through a Bit More

# Make Past Boy/Girlfriend a Current FB Friend?

opinion, this means saying "I don't" to Friending old boyfriends/girlfriends on Facebook.

### Kelli:

Having a good series of conversations with the love of your life (your hubby) about setting boundaries will help you both navigate through the graveyard of past love interests you will likely come across on Facebook.

### Jason & Kelli:

Our suggestion is to start with your husband rather than the old boyfriend. Let your husband decide if you should send the Friend Request instead of letting the ex-beau decide if he wants to accept your Friend Request. Give in to your husband's feelings rather than your own feelings.

## Related Threads:

- ▶ Ex's Profile Pic Sparks Feelings . . . . . . . . . . . . . . . . 282
- ▶ Setting Up Boundaries . . . . . . . . . . . . . . . . . . . . . . . 319
- ▶ Declining Friend Requests with Dignity . . . . . . . . . 118
- ▶ Friending Exes or Not? . . . . . . . . . . . . . . . . . . . . . . 164
- ▶ Friend Requests from Old Flame . . . . . . . . . . . . . . 179

facebook
and Your Marriage

# Ex's Profile Pic Sparks Feelings

**Seriously? Let's Think This Through a Bit More**

### Did You Know?

Firsts are "packed with deep emotional and physiological sensations...creating what psychologists call 'flash-bulb' memories. In addition, these 'firsts' drive up dopamine and norepinephrine, chemicals in the brain that basically make us feel good, tuned in, and rewarded."

**it's been 20 years since I've seen or talked to her, when I see the friend suggestion for an old girlfriend, her picture sparks some of those old feelings. I'm happily married. What gives?**

### Jason & Kelli:

You know how a certain song reminds you of a certain childhood experience, or the smell of baked cookies reminds you of grandma's house? That fond memory sparks remembrances and emotions stuck at a certain time in your life.

First crush, first kiss, first boyfriend/girlfriend, first sexual experience, first love are different times in a person's life when a memory was made and sealed with a mixture of hormones and natural chemicals.

When one sees a person who played a role in some kind of an emotional or physical bond, the brain can trigger those chemicals and hormones, which recreates those "old feelings." While you may be 36 years old, those "feelings" are stuck at age 16.

### Jason:

A lot has changed in 20 years. You are not the same person. She is not the same person. Life is not the same as it was. Don't waste time dwelling on the old memories or revisiting the past over

▶▶▶

**facebook** and Your Marriage

282

and over. See it for what it is (an old memory) and get on with your life.

### Kelli:

Your wife should be who you spend time thinking about, reflecting on and fantasizing about. She is who you should dwell on to nurture feelings that are good, healthy, and intended for marriage.

### Jason & Kelli:

So, what you have experienced is a normal human reaction. But don't misinterpret those feelings as a legitimate reason for making choices or taking steps to try to recreate the relationship that sparked that flurry of feelings. See them for what they really are and don't read into them anything more.

## Related Threads:

- Make Past Boy/Girlfriend a Current FB Friend? . . 280
- Creating Your Own Boundaries . . . . . . . . . . . . . . . 341
- Friending Exes or Not? . . . . . . . . . . . . . . . . . . . . . . 164
- Concerns with Spouse Friending Exes . . . . . . . . . 242
- Hiding, Removing & Blocking People . . . . . . . . . . 191

# Spouse Overreacting on Friend Choices

## Seriously? Let's Think This Through a Bit More

### Making a Difference

**get it together.** operationUs

Operation Us is a project to promote healthy marriages, relationships and families. Operation Us provides events and workshops for teens, single adults, or dating, married, and remarried couples.

---

**My wife is really upset that I've become FB Friends with some ex-girlfriends. How can I get her to chill out?**

### Jason & Kelli:

Have you heard the saying, "If Momma ain't happy, ain't nobody happy"?

There is a lot of truth to it. And in most cases, "Momma ain't happy" because Daddy ain't valuing her and she don't like it.

Instead of answering your original question, we're going to reframe it for you. Then we'll help you answer the reframed question so that you can have peace in your marriage.

The question you should have asked is: "Why is my wife upset that I have become FB Friends with some ex-girlfriends?"

So, what do you think? Jealousy? Insecurity? Fear? All of the above?

### Kelli:

If you didn't ask her opinion on the matter before Friending the ex-girlfriends, you can add disrespecting her to the possibilities too.

▶▶▶

**facebook** and Your Marriage

284

**Jason & Kelli:**

Hopefully you've answered the new and improved question, Here's a question for you: Is reconnecting on Facebook with old girlfriends worth creating jealousy, insecurity, and/or fear in (and possibly disrespecting) your wife?

If the answer is "yes," skip ahead to the thread on Finding Help because finding a therapist would be a really good idea. If the answer is "no," then skim back to the threads on "Hiding, Removing & Blocking People" (page 191). Regardless, set up an "About Us" date with your wife (page 334) to talk about boundaries (pages 319 and 344) for your time on Facebook.

## Related Threads:

- ▶ Having Insecurity Surges . . . . . . . . . . . . . . . . . . . . . . 238
- ▶ Concerns with Spouse Friending Exes . . . . . . . . . 242
- ▶ Spouse Broke Agreement on Friends . . . . . . . . . 245
- ▶ Setting Up Boundaries . . . . . . . . . . . . . . . . . . . . . . . 319
- ▶ Living Inbounds . . . . . . . . . . . . . . . . . . . . . . . . . . . . . 344

# Can't Wait to Facebook With Someone

## Seriously? Let's Think This Through a Bit More

### Our Book Club Picks

*Close Calls.* Dave Carder has spent thirty years counseling husbands and wives who've had affairs, and shares what heartbroken adulterers want married people to know about protecting their marriage.

I have reconnected with some old friends from high school. One of them is a guy I had a huge crush on (although we never dated). We have been emailing and chatting on Facebook daily for the last month and a half. I can't wait to get home from work and see if he's messaged me or, better yet, if he's online. I'm feeling a little guilty because I'd rather chat with him than be with my husband. But I don't want to stop either. What's going on?

**Kelli:**

You need a friend. No, you need a REAL friend. No, you need a REAL friend who is a GIRL. Your need to have someone you can talk with, share with, and relate with is healthy, appropriate, and necessary. You really need a healthy friendship with another female who you can spend time with and build a relationship with that will not threaten your marriage.

**Jason & Kelli:**

What you have established is not healthy, not safe, and frankly, not real. The fact that you're feeling some guilt shows you know it too.

Your Facebook liaison sounds like an emotional affair; a bit of fantasy mixed with attempts to meet unmet personal needs. This is a dangerous combination that will not turn out well for all those

▶▶▶

**facebook** *and Your Marriage*

directly and indirectly involved. The fact that you don't want it to stop shows you know it too.

So now that we've explained "what's going on," what are you going to do about it?

Our advice is (1) end the emotional affair immediately, (2) Block the guy, (3) talk with your husband about establishing boundaries for your Facebook time, (4) find a way to connect emotionally with your husband, and (5) find a female friend.

**Jason:**

You probably need to see a counselor too to help you figure what was so appealing and what you were getting out of this relationship that you aren't receiving from your marriage. Then start making changes so you can have a long-lasting, guilt-free affair...with your husband.

## Related Threads:

- Is It an Emotional Affair?......................254
- Concerns with Spouse Friending Exes .........242
- Ex's Profile Pic Sparks Feelings ...............282
- Hiding, Removing & Blocking People ..........191
- Finding Help...................................349

# Changing My Status to "It's Complicated"

**Seriously? Let's Think This Through a Bit More**

## Our Book Club Picks

*Can My Marriage be Saved* by Mae Chambers and Erika Chambers is filled with more than twenty true stories of couples whose marriages were restored, even after being deemed hopeless. Their stories of overcoming devastating circumstances provides hope for any troubled marriage and practical help for any couple in a similar situation.

**My husband and I are separating and I need to change my status to "It's Complicated." Where do I change my Relationship Status?**

### Jason & Kelli:

Sorry to hear that you and your husband are separating. But here's another question for you: Why do you need to change your Relationship Status if you're still married?

What do you think will happen when people see the Facebook notice that you changed your Relationship Status from "Married" to "It's Complicated"? Are you looking for attention, sympathy, or support from your FB Friends?

What do you think will happen when your husband sees the change? Will he get angry or embarrassed? Will this inspire him to make changes you want or will it further complicate the situation?

Are you ready for how people will respond to the change in your Relationship Status? You'll get everything from words of concern ("I'm sorry to hear that.") to words of criticism ("He's a jerk!") to words of curiosity ("So what happened, you seemed so happy?"). And many of these comments will be public for all Facebook eyes to see (e.g. your neighbors, co-workers, family, and your kids if they're on Facebook).

▶▶▶

**facebook** and Your Marriage

288

# Seriously? Let's Think This Through a Bit More

## Changing My Status to "It's Complicated"

**Kelli:**

Oh, and be ready for people to hit on you and on him. There's a whole bunch of opportunists out there.

**Jason & Kelli:**

Even though the two of you are separating, you are still married and that Relationship Status designation is still completely valid.

**Jason:**

And just so you know, many couples who separate and work on their relationship get back together with a stronger marriage than before the separation.

**Jason & Kelli:**

If you want to add to the level of complication by changing your status to "It's Complicated," make the change by editing your Profile page.

**Kelli:**

But do yourself, your husband, and your marriage a favor...make a positive impact in your relationship rather than a negative impact

▶▶▶

**facebook**
*and Your Marriage*

by changing your Relationship Status. Go to **FacebookAndYourMarriage.com** and find books, websites and resources aimed at helping you and your marriage. It's a little more time consuming and personally demanding than clicking an option in a drop down menu, but it gives your relationship a much better chance to improve.

## Related Threads:

- Relationship Status . . . . . . . . . . . . . . . . . . . . . . . . . . . 76
- Spouse Changed "Married" to "It's Complicated" . 264
- Spouse Spends Too Much Time on FB . . . . . . . . . 232
- Turning Screaming Matches Into Conversations . . 325
- Finding Help . . . . . . . . . . . . . . . . . . . . . . . . . . . . . . . 349

**Seriously? Let's Think This Through a Bit More**

# My Spouse is Spying on Me

**Help! My husband logged into my FB account and read some emails I exchanged with a guy from work. The emails were a little suggestive and flirty, but we were just joking with each other. I'm really upset that my husband didn't respect my privacy. How do I get him to see what he did?**

### Jason & Kelli:

Spouses are fairly perceptive and can sense when things aren't quite right.

Assuming you exchanged each other's Facebook log-in information as a gesture of trust and accountability in your relationship, what reasons would your husband have to follow through and act on that gesture of trust and accountability?

And since you admit that there are what some would consider "inappropriate" emails with someone who is not your husband, it seems that whatever suspicions motivated him to log into your Facebook account was confirmed when he read the emails.

### Jason:

Try putting yourself in your husband's shoes. You (as him) have just read emails that are "a little suggestive and flirty" written by your wife to

▶▶▶

**facebook**
*and Your Marriage*

another man. How do you feel? What effect does this have on you? What are you thinking?

Hopefully, this different vantage point gives you a new perspective to the situation.

### Jason & Kelli:

If you happen to be feeling any guilt or regret about the email exchange, address the situation with your husband, confess what you did, and ask for his forgiveness.

### Kelli:

And woman-to-woman: you should be feeling some guilt and regrets.

On your wedding day, you made a vow before God, family, and friends that you would "forsake all others" for your husband.

That doesn't mean just sex. It is anything intimate, sexual, pseudo-sexual, or flirtatious. You crossed a line and you need to own up to it and make it right.

### Jason & Kelli:

Creating some guardrails for your time and interactions on Facebook is a must to ensure

▶▶▶

you don't crash into the ditch, or worse, drive (yourself and your marriage) over the cliff. Set up some boundaries with your husband as soon as possible.

### Related Threads:

- Password Exchange . . . . . . . . . . . . . . . . . . . . . . . . 146
- Chatting Boundaries . . . . . . . . . . . . . . . . . . . . . . . . 162
- Logging Into My Mate's Facebook . . . . . . . . . . . . 251
- Setting Up Boundaries . . . . . . . . . . . . . . . . . . . . . 319
- Finding Solutions for Your FB Problems . . . . . . . 328

## Our Book Club Picks

*Private Lies* by Frank Pittman identifies four basic patterns of infidelity, discusses how to limit the damage that affairs do, and offers practical suggestions on how to make a marriage work.

**Recently I've been emailing and chatting with an old boyfriend who I reconnected with through Facebook. It feels like we picked up right where we left off. We have this deep emotional connection and used to have great physical chemistry. I wasn't looking for this, but it found me. I love my husband, but I feel so complete when I Facebook with my ex-boyfriend. I never planned for this, but I am seriously considering leaving my husband. It's OK if I'm following my heart, right?**

### Jason & Kelli:

We're not big fans of people "following their heart." Especially when one's "heart" is leading them into a high-risk situation that will likely blow up and cause a person to lose everything that matters most.

### Jason:

Some never reach the destination they think their heart is leading them to.

### Jason & Kelli:

When it comes to old love interests, former boyfriends or girlfriends, or past sexual partners, while there was an attraction, a shared experience,

▶▶▶

294

or a series of fond memories at one point in time, it's important to realize what is and is not going on now.

What is going on? When you're interacting with a "special" person from your past, your brain is recalling a flood of memories associated with this person. Those memories draw us in and can keep us there because of the feelings (all of the positive feelings and very little of the negative feelings) associated with this person and the nostalgia of that season of life you were in at that time. The two of you are likely immersing yourselves in those feelings and misinterpreting them as "love."

What is not going on? Your relationship with this person is based on the past, not the present. Your remembrances are more of a fantasy of what once was than the reality of your shared past. It's like the negative parts (arguments, differences, break-up) are being air-brushed to look better, sound nicer, and feel greater than what really occurred. Present-day reality, rationality, and relationships are not a part of the equation as you two reminisce.

What parts of your life could continue as-is if you leave your marriage for this guy? Could you keep your job? Would your day-to-day life and daily conveniences continue as is? What would your kids and/or your extended family think of you?

If you were to make the jump from your marriage to this Facebook-inspired hook-up, what would the next steps of the relationship be? Meet him face-to-face? Introduce him to family and kids? Meet his kids and family? Move closer to him or he moves closer to you? Marry each other once your divorces are finalized? What would stepfamily life look like?

What effect would taking any further step in this guy's direction have on every important relationship in your life? With your current spouse? Your family? Your in-laws? Your kids? Your friends? Your co-workers?

Spend a lot of time thinking through these questions before you take any action. As best as you can, separate reality from the nostalgia. And before you make any regrettable decisions, talk this through with a good friend, a trusted family member, or your minister or priest and give them permission to ask you the hard questions.

**Kelli:**

You wrote that "it found me." Guess what, "It " is unable to search and find anyone because "It " isn't a living thing. You opened yourself to a situation and to someone that allowed this to happen. (And at the same time, you closed yourself to self-control, self-discipline, and personal integrity.) You should really try to figure out why you put yourself and your marriage in such a vulnerable spot. A journal, a friend, a pastor, and a counselor could help a lot with this.

▶▶▶

**Seriously? Let's Think This Through a Bit More**

**Rekindled Romance on Facebook**

**Jason & Kelli:**

Hopefully, you'll come to the point where you get back to reality, end the exchanges with this guy by Blocking him, and pour yourself into the relationship that really matters...the one where you exchanged vows and committed to faithfully love "'til death do you part."

## Related Threads:

- ▶ Friending Exes or Not?........................164
- ▶ Finding Help..................................349
- ▶ Hiding, Removing & Blocking People..........191
- ▶ Concerns with Spouse Friending Exes.........242
- ▶ Is It an Emotional Affair?..................254

**facebook**
*and Your Marriage*

# From Facebook to Face-to-Face

## Seriously? Let's Think This Through a Bit More

### Our Book Club Picks

*Hedges* by Jerry Jenkins teaches readers how to plant preventative hedges around their marriage, helping spouses avoid compromising situations and not give in to temptation. Through real-life stories, learn how temptation works, watch the dizzying whirl of betrayal, and hear what other marriages have had to go through to survive.

---

I am not sure what to do. I am happily married and a new dad. A few months ago my ex-fiancee (who called off our engagement five years ago) found me on Facebook and we've emailed and chatted a few times. She wants to meet up and I would like to see her, but I know my wife would flip out. Part of me thinks it's a bad idea, but I really want to share with her face-to-face how her calling off the engagement hurt me. Can you give me some advice here?

### Jason & Kelli:

If all you're looking for is some closure with this woman, the question is how can the route to closure be safe for you, your wife, and your marriage?

The first step is to talk with your wife. Does she know about the emails and chat exchanges on Facebook? Would you be comfortable if she read your emails to and from the ex-fiancee? Will your wife be comfortable about the private conversations you're having with the ex? How would she feel about you having a face-to-face meeting?

If your wife is not supportive, the idea is dead in the water. To help with the closure issue, find a counselor who can help you work through some of the past hurt.

▶▶▶

facebook and Your Marriage

**Seriously? Let's Think This Through a Bit More**

If your spouse green-lights the idea, the meeting should be a onetime occurrence between you, the woman, and a male friend of yours. Your friend's presence is a MUST-HAVE for this meeting.

Prior to the meeting, write out a script or outline of what you're planning on sharing. Get your wife's approval on it. Keep the conversation on topic and according to the script, with the focus to bring about closure. Do not spend time reminiscing about old times. Arrive with your friend and leave with your friend.

Regardless if the meeting for closure occurs, we recommend that there be a cease-and-desist order on all communications with the ex-fiancee. Block her and call it all good.

After the meeting, give your wife a detailed blow-by-blow of the conversation. Let her ask any question she has, and offer her any information she wants.

After you're done reporting how the meeting went, finish the conversation by expressing your commitment to her and your marriage, and declare that this past relationship is over, done, finished, and officially deceased.

**Kelli:**

In fact, kick off this new season in your marriage with a class or workshop that will forge a stronger bond between you and your wife. Find a whole lot of potential programs at **FacebookAndYourMarriage.com**.

**Jason:**

All this advice was sparked off your statement that indicated you wanted and needed closure. If there is anything in your head or heart flirting with the idea of something more happening here (desire to see her, hoping to rekindle something, etc), then you need to Stop, Drop and Roll. Stop the exchanges with her immediately. Drop her as a FB Friend by Blocking her. Roll and smother yourself in resources to strengthen your marriage and learn to love your wife as she deserves to be loved.

## Related Threads:

- Ex-Spouse OK as FB Friend? . . . . . . . . . . . . . . . . . .268
- Is It an Emotional Affair? . . . . . . . . . . . . . . . . . . . . .254
- Am I About to Have an Affair? . . . . . . . . . . . . . . . . 301
- Working Through Infidelity Together . . . . . . . . .346
- Finding Help . . . . . . . . . . . . . . . . . . . . . . . . . . . . . . . .349

# Seriously? Let's Think This Through a Bit More

# Am I About to Have an Affair?

**Tomorrow I am meeting a man face-to-face I met on FB a few months back. We have so much in common, play the same games, etc., and I really enjoy chatting with him on Facebook. We've even talked on the phone a few times. We seem to have more in common than my husband and I do. We're just friends, but I'm a little nervous about where things could go. Thoughts?**

### Jason & Kelli:

Sounds like your conscience is trying to get through to you. And if you're not willing to listen to that inner voice that's attempted to steer you toward good, healthy, and safe decisions your entire life, maybe you'll listen to an expert on affairs, the late Shirley Glass.

In her book *Not "Just Friends,"* Glass raises three red flags that separate platonic friendships from romantic emotional affairs.

The first red flag is *emotional intimacy*. The two parties share "personal things about their hopes and fears," and turn to each other to "discuss troubling aspects of their marriage(s)." They act like "soul mates and best friends," leaving their spouse(s) "in the shadows like half-remembered dreams."

The second red flag is *secrecy*. By creating a "world well away from the pressure, responsibilities, and routines of ordinary family life," the relationship

### It's Been Said

*"Infidelity occurs when one partner in a relationship continues to believe that the agreement to be faithful is still in force, while the other partner is secretly violating it."*

Dr. Don-David Lusterman, author of Infidelity: A Survival Guide

▶▶▶

**facebook**
*and Your Marriage*

# Am I About to Have an Affair?

## Seriously? Let's Think This Through a Bit More

increases with "intensity and (is) fueled (by) their preoccupation with each other."

The third red flag is *sexual chemistry*. Simply put, this is "inflamed by forbidden sex" that is fueled by the two parties' fantasies about a sexual relationship "even though they agreed that they would never act on their mutual desire. But in suppressing it, they (find) the sexual tension being deliciously increased."

How many of these red flags are standing at full mast in your relationship with this guy?

### Jason:

Most of these relationships don't last long, they rarely lead to something more permanent, and deliver a whole lot of pain, guilt and shame.

### Kelli:

Don't do it!!! The fact that you are questioning this means you know it is wrong. Block this guy and turn your desires and focus onto your husband. He'll receive your affections and your love and return them in a way this other guy never could. Then get some counseling for yourself. You need some help when it comes to setting up boundaries...on and off of Facebook.

# Seriously? Let's Think This Through a Bit More

# Am I About to Have an Affair?

**Jason & Kelli:**

It's not too late to call off the rendezvous. The regrets you'll feel from canceling the encounter are nothing compared to the regrets you'll feel if you don't.

## Related Threads:

- ▶ Leaving My Marriage . . . . . . . . . . . . . . . . . . . . . . . . 304
- ▶ Is It an Emotional Affair? . . . . . . . . . . . . . . . . . . . . . 254
- ▶ Confronting Spouse About Affair . . . . . . . . . . . . 260
- ▶ Creating Your Own Boundaries . . . . . . . . . . . . . . 341
- ▶ Finding Help . . . . . . . . . . . . . . . . . . . . . . . . . . . . . . . . 349

**facebook** and Your Marriage

# Leaving My Marriage

## Seriously? Let's Think This Through a Bit More

**Making a Difference**

**INVERSE MINISTRIES**

Inverse Ministries helps reconcile broken marriages across the nation through programs and seminars and linking people with resources that help further their reconciliation.

---

I have left my wife. I am divorcing her for the love of my life who I found thanks to Facebook. While it pains me that my wife will probably get full custody of our kids and I'll see them less and less, I have to follow my feelings. What's the best way to break this to my kids?

### Jason & Kelli:

While the phrase "I'm following my feelings" sounds pure and romantic, it is based on your immediate emotions, which are neither logical nor rational. In fact, they're so illogical and irrational, they'll lead you astray. Some would even say your emotions can and do lie to you.

So let's throw a little rational thinking into the mix. Is what you gain from this decision to leave your family for your mistress worth the pain and damage that you will inflict on your kids and your wife? How are your kids going to look back on this moment 20 years from now? Will they remember this as an act their dad made to follow his heart or as an act that broke their hearts?

### Jason:

My dad did something like this. It forever changed the relationship he had with his sons. He missed my graduations from high school and college, my wedding, and the birth of his first and second grandchildren. My dad never got what he was

▶▶▶

**facebook** and Your Marriage

looking to get when he left my mom and our family. As a child of divorce, I just want to say that you are about to take the biggest step of selfishness you can make and it will not turn out the way you think it will.

**Kelli:**

Michele Weiner-Davis writes in the introduction of her book *The Divorce Remedy*, "(E)arly in my career, like many therapists, I assumed that if people were unhappy in their marriages they should just get out.... But I soon learned the truth about divorce. It doesn't necessarily bring happiness. In fact, in most cases, divorce creates more problems than it solves."

**Jason & Kelli:**

For the sake of your kids and before you throw everything away, give your marriage another 180 days.

Over the course of the next 180 days, take the following seven steps:

1. Write down two lists. One is what your life will be like if you stay and work on your marriage. The second is what your life will be like if you leave the marriage. Don't just think of the immediate future; think 10 to 30 years down the road of what your life

will really look like. Add to your lists and change your lists over the 180 days.

2. Take a 30-day fast from the relationship with your new Facebook "love." After the first 30 days, see where your feelings are for her. Then take another 30-day fast.

3. On your own, meet with a counselor or go see your clergy. Meet with one or both weekly during the 180 days.

4. Read two to three books about the affects of divorce on kids (*Between Two Worlds: The Inner Lives of Children of Divorce* by Elizabeth Marquardt is a suggestion; more book titles are listed at **FacebookAndYourMarriage.com**).

5. Read two to three books on how to work on your marriage (*Divorce Busting* by Michele Weiner-Davis is just one book we recommend; more book suggestions at **FacebookAndYourMarriage.com**).

6. Meet with a marriage therapist with your wife a minimum of six times.

7. Spend time with your kids weekly. Build up the quality of your relationship by talking with them instead of just going off to have fun little excursions.

As a bonus, you might try attending a relationship class or a marriage enrichment program. Some allow for spouses to come without a mate, while others don't. Either way, you can learn some amazing relationship skills that can make all the difference in a marriage.

After the 180 days, see where your head, your heart, and your desires are at.

**Jason:**

My bet is that you'll have a different perspective than you do right now, one that's really best for your kids!

## Related Threads:

- ▶ The "About Us" Date . . . . . . . . . . . . . . . . . . . . . . .334
- ▶ Working Through Infidelity Together . . . . . . . . . .346
- ▶ Is Our Marriage Over? . . . . . . . . . . . . . . . . . . . . . . 271
- ▶ Repairing a Marriage I Messed Up . . . . . . . . . . . .308
- ▶ Finding Help. . . . . . . . . . . . . . . . . . . . . . . . . . . . . .349

# Repairing a Marriage I Messed Up

### Seriously? Let's Think This Through a Bit More

**I've messed up! For the last several months I have been having an affair with an ex-boyfriend I connected with on Facebook. I've ended it and want to fix my relationship with my husband. Where do I go from here?**

### Jason & Kelli:

Infidelity does not have to be the death knell in a marriage. Many couples have overcome the pain of adultery and repaired their marriage, oftentimes making it stronger and healthier than ever.

But before the healing can begin, the affair must be completely over. Have you Blocked the ex-boyfriend (and any other exes, past love interests, and crushes) from your list of FB Friends? You must!

Before talking to your husband, do some looking on the inside to try to find out why you did what you did. When he asks, "Why?" you need to have a better answer than "I don't know." You don't have to have it all figured out, but try to identify why you went down this road in the first place. Was it emotional or physical needs, relationship issues, a lack of boundaries, or something else?

**facebook** and Your Marriage

**Seriously? Let's Think This Through a Bit More**

**Repairing a Marriage I Messed Up**

**Kelli:**

Journaling or talking with someone could help you sort through your feelings, emotions, and pain.

**Jason:**

As you sort out your actions, do not make your husband the reason why you did what you did (e.g. "If only you would do this," or "I wouldn't have strayed if I got more attention from you".) Also, don't make the ex-beau a scapegoat to justify your actions either (e.g. "He took advantage of me," or "He made me feel a certain way".) You need to own your actions. You made the decision to stray, so you owe it to your husband to take the lead to repair the marriage.

**Jason & Kelli:**

Set up an "About Us" date with your husband and be prepared to share, to cry, to feel shame, and to listen. He needs to know that (1) it's over, (2) you've taken steps to remove the person from your life, (3) you're taking responsibility for your actions, (4) you're committed to your marriage, and (5) you're seeking his forgiveness.

Your husband will likely have a hard time with this. He will need time and space to grapple with

▶▶▶

his own feelings, to deal with his insecurities, and to rebuild trust in you.

You'll likely have your own emotional stuff to get through, including guilt, grief, and shame.

This is the kind of situation where a third party can really help you two: a marriage therapist, a pastor, or a marriage organization that specializes in couple reconciliation after infidelity. Find a list of many that we greatly respect and admire at **FacebookAndYourMarriage.com**.

### Related Threads:

- Spouse Wants a Do-Over . . . . . . . . . . . . . . . . . . . . . 274
- The "About Us" Date . . . . . . . . . . . . . . . . . . . . . . 334
- Creating Your Own Boundaries . . . . . . . . . . . . . . 341
- Working Through Infidelity Together . . . . . . . . . 346
- Finding Help . . . . . . . . . . . . . . . . . . . . . . . . . . . . . 349

## Section 9

*Facebook is a part of our lives. Therefore, it is a part of our marriage life too. Facebook should be something all couples should talk about...in real time. This thread set gives couples everything they need to make their conversations and conflicts as stress-free and solution-based as possible using communication tools and skills guaranteed to make their time on Facebook safer and their marriage stronger.*

- ▸ Talking Without Fighting . . . . . . . . . . . . . . . . . . . . . . . . . . . . 314
- ▸ Setting Up Boundaries . . . . . . . . . . . . . . . . . . . . . . . . . . . . . . 319
- ▸ Resolving Conflict Quickly. . . . . . . . . . . . . . . . . . . . . . . . . . . 322
- ▸ Turning Screaming Matches Into Conversations . . . . . . . 325
- ▸ Finding Solutions for Your FB Problems. . . . . . . . . . . . . . . 328
- ▸ Uh-Huh Is Never Enough . . . . . . . . . . . . . . . . . . . . . . . . . . . 331
- ▸ The "About Us" Date . . . . . . . . . . . . . . . . . . . . . . . . . . . . . . .334
- ▸ Calling for an "About Us" Date. . . . . . . . . . . . . . . . . . . . . . 338
- ▸ Creating Your Own Boundaries . . . . . . . . . . . . . . . . . . . . . 341
- ▸ Living Inbounds. . . . . . . . . . . . . . . . . . . . . . . . . . . . . . . . . . .344
- ▸ Working Through Infidelity Together . . . . . . . . . . . . . . . .346
- ▸ Finding Help. . . . . . . . . . . . . . . . . . . . . . . . . . . . . . . . . . . . . .349

# TMI! Talking With Your Mate Offline About Online Issues

# Talking Without Fighting

## TMI! Talking with Your Mate Offline About Online Issues

### Making a Difference

**The Oklahoma Marriage Initiative** is one of the nation's first statewide efforts providing couples communication and conflict resolution classes throughout Oklahoma.

The tension in our home is really thick right now. My wife constantly complains that I spend too much time playing multi-player games online. But when I remind her I spend no more time on my games than she does playing her Facebook games, we end up getting into a huge fight. Is there any help you could pass our way?

**Jason & Kelli:**

Before you can do things right, it is important to know what you're doing wrong. While you two are playing different games on the computer, it sounds like you're playing similar Fighting Games in real life.

**Jason:**

In my premarital book, *Before "I Do,"* couples learn about the four most common ways people deal with conflict in a relationship. They're adapted (with permission) from a list of fighting styles in the PREP program by Scott Stanley and Howard Markman. And in the game of "love and marriage," people play some, all, or a combination of the Four Fighting Games with each other.

**facebook** *and Your Marriage*

### Jason & Kelli:

The first Fighting Game is called **Verbal Tug-of-War**. This happens when each spouse anchors themselves on opposing sides and *"negatively responds toward one another in a verbal give-and-take match causing the conversation to escalate."*

### Acting Wife:

You're always on Facebook. Get off the computer and do something around the house.

### Acting Husband:

Well, you're one to talk! If you would spend less time playing games on Facebook, maybe we could eat a meal that isn't cooked by a microwave.

### Jason & Kelli:

The second Fighting Game is **Put Down Tag**. When one spouse possesses *"the self-appointed responsibility of 'being it'"* they *"directly or indirectly put down the other partner's character, abilities, appearance, ideas, thoughts, or feelings."*

# Talking Without Fighting

## TMI! Talking with Your Mate Offline About Online Issues

**Acting Husband:**

Do you really think people care what you write on Facebook? The people reading it are probably as desperate for friends as you are. Losers!

**Jason & Kelli:**

The third Fighting Game is **Conspiracy Poker**. This occurs when a spouse makes up their own house rules and "creates a conspiracy in their mind about the motives, thoughts, and actions of their mate. Instead of confronting their partner by 'laying down their cards,' they continue to 'deal new hands" that support their own suspicions and hunches.

**Acting Wife:**

You probably just got on Facebook because you're afraid I'm having too good of a time and you just want to check on me.

**Acting Husband:**

No, I got on Facebook because our reunion is coming up and this is how they're sending out the information.

▶▶▶

### facebook and Your Marriage

### Acting Wife:

We're in the same graduating class. You could have just relied on me to give you the info. You are so checking on me! You just don't trust me.

### Jason & Kelli:

The final Fighting Game is **Conflict Hide-and-Go-Seek**. "*This game begins when one partner withdraws (hides) from a conversation about conflict, avoids the discussion all together, tends to get quiet during an argument, quickly agrees to prematurely end the conversation, or avoids allowing the discussion to occur at all. This can cause the other partner to pursue (seek) the discussion, the conflict, and the partner.*"

### Acting Wife:

Come out from your man-cave! I've got a gripe, which means we have issues. We need to deal with it now!

### Acting Husband:

I'm really busy uploading pictures to Facebook and my computer is taking forever to load them. We'll need to talk later.

## Our Book Club Picks

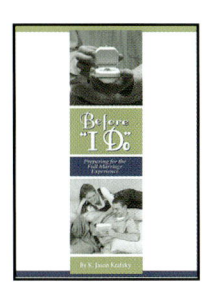

*Before "I Do"* provides seriously dating, engaged and newly married couples with the skills and insights to live the full marriage experience.

### Jason & Kelli:

There is a winner and a loser in every game people play. But when it comes to the Four Fighting Games, regardless of who "wins" the argument, both the husband and the wife end up losing.

### Kelli:

Sounds like there may be a little Verbal Tug-of-War going on with you and your wife. Now that you know what you're doing wrong, be sure to read the Related Threads to discover what you need to do to handle conflict right.

## Related Threads:

- ▸ Avoiding FB Addiction . . . . . . . . . . . . . . . . . . . . . . . 148
- ▸ Spouse Spends Too Much Time on FB . . . . . . . . . 232
- ▸ Resolving Conflict Quickly . . . . . . . . . . . . . . . . . . 322
- ▸ Turning Screaming Matches Into Conversations . . 325
- ▸ Uh-Huh Is Never Enough . . . . . . . . . . . . . . . . . . . 331

# Setting Up Boundaries

**TMI! Talking with Your Mate Offline About Online Issues**

A friend of mine says she and her husband have something called boundaries they've agreed to follow when they're on Facebook. Things like not friending old boyfriends or girlfriends. I think this could be good for my husband and me, but I'm not sure how to explain boundaries to him. Can you give me some talking points?

**Jason & Kelli:**

Setting up personal boundaries is a part of everyday life. In neighborhoods, homes are built on land with definite property lines. A fence or hedge is often used to clearly identify the property line. But the fence also acts as a definite boundary; a protection for those within the property line (say a toddler playing in the backyard) and a protective barrier from threats outside of the property line (like a stray dog).

In relationships with friends, co-workers, clients, family members, and strangers, we have relational "property lines" that must be identified and protected by boundaries. Boundaries are the personal set of rules we follow to protect ourselves physically, emotionally, spiritually, and relationally.

Boundaries in marriage start on the wedding day (vowing to monogamy, committing to care for each other regardless of circumstances, and legally and permanently changing the relationship status to husband and wife). But more boundaries

▶▶▶

## Transform Your Relationship

PREP (Prevention and Relationship Enhancement Program) is one of the most comprehensive and respected divorce-prevention/marriage enhancing programs in the world. PREP is a skills and principles-building curriculum designed to help partners say what they need to say, get to the heart of problems, and increase their connection with each other.

**facebook and Your Marriage**

# Setting Up Boundaries

## TMI! Talking with Your Mate Offline About Online Issues

are needed to proactively protect yourself, your spouse, your marriage, your family.

In a book called Boundaries in Marriage, the authors talk about the triangle of boundaries (freedom, responsibility, and love). "Something incredible happens as these three ingredients of relationship work together. As love grows, spouses become more free from the things that enslave: self-centeredness, singular patterns, past hurts, and other self-imposed limitations. Then, they gain a greater and greater sense of self-control and responsibility. As they act more responsibly, they become more loving. And then the cycle begins all over again. As love grows, so does freedom, leading to more responsibility, and to more love."

**Jason:**

One of the boundaries we set up as a perimeter around our relationship (before we got married) is that neither of us would be alone with someone of the opposite sex. Not because we are worried about the other cheating, but to avoid the appearance of impropriety or being caught in a potential he said/she said situation. We've heard too many stories of how an accusation (some true, some false) has tarnished a reputation or ended a career. A simple boundary could have saved a lot of anguish and pain.

▶▶▶

**facebook**
*and Your Marriage*

# TMI! Talking with Your Mate Offline About Online Issues

## Setting Up Boundaries

**Jason & Kelli:**

Understanding your personal boundaries and agreeing to shared boundaries creates a heavy-duty protection around the marriage.

**Kelli:**

In virtual spaces, it is really important for couples to be on the same page about what is and is not appropriate. Unfortunately, too many couples assume they're on the same page until it's too late and they find out that they're not even on the same bookshelf.

**Jason:**

Spend time defining your "property lines" and erecting "a fence" for your time on Facebook.

### Related Threads:

- ▶ Creating Your Own Boundaries . . . . . . . . . . . . . . . 341
- ▶ Living Inbounds . . . . . . . . . . . . . . . . . . . . . . . . . . . 344
- ▶ Friending Exes…or Not? . . . . . . . . . . . . . . . . . . . . . 164
- ▶ Chatting Boundaries . . . . . . . . . . . . . . . . . . . . . . . 162
- ▶ Spouse Broke Agreement on Friends . . . . . . . . . 245

**facebook** and Your Marriage

321

# Resolving Conflict Quickly

## TMI! Talking with Your Mate Offline About Online Issues

### Our Book Club Picks

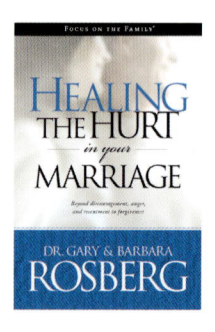

*Healing the Hurt in Your Marriage* by Dr. Gary and Barbara Rosberg provides you with an excellent examination of conflict and a practical step-by-step process for resolving it in a healthy manner. Learn how to close the loop that can help heal hurts, improve communication, foster forgiveness, promote trust and build a sound marriage.

**Can you help me out here? I'm totally in support of setting boundaries for Facebook and my wife and I have set some up. I sometimes write stupid things on Facebook that offend her or accidentally put her down. A simple "I'm sorry" is not enough for her. We end up having these marathon discussions about her feelings. It makes me want to scrap FB altogether.**

### Jason & Kelli:

Over the course of a marriage, husbands and wives will have ample opportunities to say the wrong thing at the wrong time. Many times, one spouse is oblivious that they've offended the other.

The unfortunate reality with Facebook is when we post something stupid in an update or making a comment, it's out there for all our FB Friends to read and respond to.

Marriage is a 24/7 living arrangement between two people. There are ample opportunities to say something without thinking that will unintentionally offend one's spouse. When this kind of thing happens (whether it's on Facebook or in real-time), couples need to have a quick and easy way to address and resolve the offense.

Luckily for all of us spouses, some smart people came up with an easy-to-remember tool to help

▶▶▶

## facebook
### and Your Marriage

us swiftly deal with an issue without killing an evening.

**Kelli:**

Or each other. LOL

**Jason & Kelli:**

The XYZ Statement should be in every couple's toolbox. It is an easy to remember structure to share a grievance without blowing the whole thing out of proportion. It goes like this:

"When you do X…" (a specific behavior)

"…in situation Y…" (a specific situation)

"…I feel Z." (a specific feeling)

This is how it would work in your scenario. You post something stupid like, "Something must have crawled into my wife's mouth last night and died! She has the worst morning breath." Your wife reads your update and is predictably upset. Rather than stewing on it and getting madder and madder throughout the day, she comes to you and pulls an XYZ.

*"Honey, when you post an embarrassing message about me (X) and post it for all your Facebook Friends to read (Y) I feel humiliated (Z)."*

**Jason:**

This is where you man up by acknowledging her concern, taking responsibility for your actions, and apologizing to her. End of story. If you really blew it, remove the post or comment, apologize to her on Facebook wherever the "stupid post" was posted, and then post something nice and affirming about her.

**Kelli:**

By the way, to avoid this in the future, read your post out loud before sharing it with all of Facebook. It will save you and your spouse a lot of grief.

## Related Threads:

- Turning Screaming Matches Into Conversations . . 325
- Talking Without Fighting . . . . . . . . . . . . . . . . . . . . . . 314
- When Private Stuff Goes Public . . . . . . . . . . . . . . . . 186
- Finding Solutions for Your FB Problems . . . . . . . 328
- Creating Your Own Boundaries . . . . . . . . . . . . . . . 341

# TMI! Talking with Your Mate Offline About Online Issues

## Turning Screaming Matches Into Conversations

**When I try to talk with my husband about some of his choices for FB Friends, it turns into a screaming match. We love each other, but we also know how to push each other's buttons. How am I ever going to be able to tell him my concerns without it turning into a war of words?**

### Jason & Kelli:

We possess twice as many body parts designed for listening than those for talking, but somehow that doesn't make much of a difference for couples. We tend to over-think, under-listen, and out-talk our spouse when pride or ego is on the line.

### Kelli:

So, the secret to a scream-free exchange is to slow down the conversation.

### Jason & Kelli:

You have probably heard of active listening or a special variation of it found in most every communication program. The goal is not to learn how to speak or listen better. The ultimate goal is to better understand the other person, where they're coming from, what they think and most importantly, how they feel.

---

**Making a Difference**

The Healthy Marriage Coalition of Fresno/Madera County offers couples classes and relationship skills programs designed to help couples learn communication skills in the class and apply them in day-to-day life.

▶▶▶

**facebook** *and Your Marriage*

So get your husband, set up some of the following guidelines, and begin a conflict-free conversation. (This particular set of guidelines is from the Speaker-Listener Technique from our friends at PREP who also happen to be the authors of *Fighting for Your Marriage*.)

To start off, one spouse has a physical object (a remote, a computer mouse, a video game controller) in their hand to designate who the Speaker is.

### Jason:

The PREP folks call it "the Floor" (it's a long story).

### Jason & Kelli:

The Speaker starts the conversation, speaking in short chunks of a sentence or two. The other spouse (the Listener) listens and paraphrases back what they heard. There's no interpreting, no responding, and no debating. The conversation continues this way until the Speaker has said everything he needs to say.

At that point, the Listener takes "the Floor" and becomes the Speaker. He then gets to share following the same prescription above.

While it sounds overly simplistic and may feel a little robotic at first, the results can be astounding!

**Jason:**

I have heard from a number of couples that this type of process has helped them avoid a World War III type of fight.

**Kelli:**

When the focus is to better understand your mate's wants and needs rather than winning the argument, everything changes...everything.

## Related Threads:

- ▶ Talking Without Fighting.....................314
- ▶ Finding Solutions for Your FB Problems........328
- ▶ Concerns with Spouse Friending Exes .........242
- ▶ Spouse Overreacting on Friend Choices .......284
- ▶ Setting Up Boundaries........................319

# Finding Solutions for Your FB Problems

### TMI! Talking with Your Mate Offline About Online Issues

## Our Book Club Picks

*Fighting for Your Marriage* by Dr. Howard Markman, Scott Stanley and Susan Blumberg provides couples with the fundamentals they need to communicate and overcome conflict. Based on the nationally recognized Prevention and Relationship Enhancement Program.

---

**My wife and I have a problem we need to solve, and soon. We both admit we're addicted to Facebook! What kinds of advice do you have for us as we will be talking about it tonight after work?**

### Jason & Kelli:

Congratulations! Not on the part of being Facebook addicts, but on your decision to move beyond talking about the problem and trying to solve the issue.

Many couples embark on the quest to have a productive conversation with high hopes, only to find themselves neck deep in the quicksand of hurt feelings, unrealistic expectations, and differences of opinions because they were under prepared for the journey of problem solving.

It starts with discussing the problem without jumping straight to problem solving.

### Kelli:

If you feel like you need help discussing the problem, be sure to check out the related threads: "Resolving Conflict Quickly," "Turning Screaming Matches Into Conversations" and "Uh-Huh is Never Enough."

▶▶▶

**facebook** and Your Marriage

328

## TMI! Talking with Your Mate Offline About Online Issues

## Finding Solutions for Your FB Problems

**Jason:**

After reading those threads, ask yourselves the following questions. Why are you both spending so much time on Facebook? What needs are being met on Facebook that aren't being met in real life? What impact is Facebook having on your relationship? What do you want and need from each other?

**Jason & Kelli:**

Then after the problem is fully discussed, it's time to discuss the solution.

First, set an agenda by picking a specific piece of the issue you want to solve. In your case it may be setting limits on the amount of time you each spend on Facebook.

Next, brainstorm ideas without criticizing or evaluating the ideas...you're just capturing the ideas. For you, it may include a range of ideas, including setting a timer, each of you going on Facebook only every other day, and shutting down the computer at a certain time in the evening.

Next, sift through your list of ideas and try to find a solution you both can live with. In other words, compromise. It is up to you to figure out what will work for the two of you, but more importantly figure out which idea (or ideas) will help you accomplish your ultimate goal: setting limits on the amount of time you spend on Facebook.

### facebook and Your Marriage

Give it a try for a couple of weeks and see if it works. If so, keep it up. If not, try another idea. This is not a process that is complete in one sitting. It may take several times to walk through and talk through the matter completely. But in the end, you will have walked and talked about the problem and its solution…together.

### Related Threads:

- Talking Without Fighting .................... 314
- Setting Up Boundaries ..................... 319
- The "About Us" Date ....................... 334
- Turning Screaming Matches Into Conversations. 325
- Uh-Huh is Never Enough .................... 331

# TMI! Talking with Your Mate Offline About Online Issues

## Uh-Huh Is Never Enough

So my wife and I have talked about Facebook. When she shared some of her concerns, I responded with an "OK" and nodding my head to let her know I heard what she was saying. After 20 minutes of talking, she got upset with me, saying I wasn't really hearing her. What gives?

**Jason & Kelli:**

In case you missed the hundreds of books aimed at describing how different men and women are, we've got news for you...men and women are different; especially when it comes to talking and listening.

But, with all the differences, what the two genders do share is a deep-seated desire to be understood by their mate.

Being understood goes beyond knowing your mate's favorite color or their daily routine. To be understood is to connect with your mate at the deepest level ...the heart level. It is sharing in the thoughts and feelings and experiences of your spouse by getting into their shoes and viewing the situation, the problem, the issue, as if you were them.

It changes everything. The "uh-huh's" turn to "oh's" as showing empathy flicks the switch that turns on the light bulb of understanding.

### Our Book Club Picks

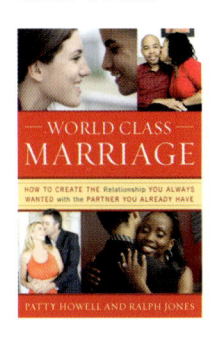

*World Class Marriage* is an engaging, practical and personal guide for relationship success written by two marriage and relationship educators who share a loving 30-year marriage with each other. Combining the latest and best information and guidance about how couples can avoid relationship damage and create lasting love.

**facebook** *and Your Marriage*

331

**Kelli:**

Go to your wife and ask for a re-do on the conversation. This time, as she shares, put yourself in her shoes.

Try to think and feel the problem from her perspective. Express back to her what she is feeling based on her own words. Don't critique it, don't explain it, and don't try to fix it. Just share what you're hearing (and seeing) from her vantage point. I guarantee, the results will be much different.

**Jason:**

For a guy, trying to get into our wife's shoes can be really difficult. We want to fix things, not relive them. We want to bring the conversation to a quick finish, not spend time reflecting on feelings and dwell on the issue. But there is no better way for a husband to love his wife than to connect with her at a heart level.

This can only be accomplished by taking the time and expending the energy to show her that you understand her and empathize with how she's feeling.

**Jason & Kelli:**

Replacing your "OK's" and nodding head with thoughtful and reflective responses, she will never again accuse you of not "hearing her."

### Related Threads:

- ▶ Talking Without Fighting......................314
- ▶ Resolving Conflict Quickly ...................322
- ▶ Turning Screaming Matches into Conversations..325
- ▶ Finding Solutions for Your FB Problems.......328
- ▶ Finding Help................................349

# The "About Us" Date

**TMI! Talking with Your Mate Offline About Online Issues**

## Making a Difference

**FIRST things FIRST**

First Things First (FTF) strengthens marriages and families through education, collaboration and mobilization. With relationship resources for everyone (young and old, married or not), FTF is making a significant difference in in reducing divorce, teen sexual activity, and fatherlessness.

### What is an "About Us" date?

**Jason & Kelli:**

Have you ever brought up an issue with your spouse, and it was the wrong time? Either your mate wasn't ready for the type of discussion you were ready to have, or your conversation was interrupted by the kids or a phone call? This is the "why" behind an "About Us" date.

**Jason:**

Early in our marriage, I turned a perfect romantic date (great meal, movie, and spending time together) into an unromantic disaster by bringing up a concern about the credit card on the ride home. While it was a valid concern, the timing was awful. In less than thirty seconds, what had taken a few hours to create completely unraveled into a stress-filled, emotionally-charged situation.

**Jason & Kelli:**

An "About Us" date is when a couple designates a special, interruption-free time to meet and discuss their relationship or issues related to their relationship (e.g. money, sex, parenting). This

▶▶▶

**facebook** and Your Marriage

can occur weekly, twice a month, monthly, or quarterly.

**Kelli:**

Had we known about it then, Jason could have set up the "About Us" date to talk over the credit card issue and saved our date date for having fun and spending time loving on one another.

**Jason & Kelli:**

The "About Us" date is the equivalent of a weekly staff meeting most every company has with its workforce. While they're not always fun, these types of meetings keep all the moving parts of the workplace up-to-date and on the same page. Sometimes there are issues to resolve, delicate topics to broach, or problems to solve. The goal of such meetings is to keep the team as unified, encouraged, and informed as possible.

**Jason:**

This should be the same goal for the "About Us" date.

# The "About Us" Date

**TMI! Talking with Your Mate Offline About Online Issues**

**Jason & Kelli:**

At the "About Us" date, both husband and wife are mentally and emotionally ready to give each other the time and attention they need to have a meaningful "About Us" dialogue.

**Kelli:**

A good rule of thumb is for the meeting to go no longer than 60 minutes.

**Jason:**

And just like any good meeting, set up a brief agenda to capture discussion items before you get started. If you don't get to a complete solution on all of them, that's OK. Keep the list (and add to it) for your next "About Us" date.

**Jason & Kelli:**

The "About Us" date can focus on an urgent matter or something more long-term. It can be an impromptu discussion, or include books, resources, or couple's studies to keep the conversation focused on the matter at hand.

Because the "About Us" date is about the two of you, it is up to the two of you to decide what needs to be discussed.

▶▶▶

**facebook** and Your Marriage

336

With the "About Us" date being on the calendar, personal stress and worry will be greatly reduced, marital friction is decreased, and family drama is greatly diminished.

## Related Threads:

▶ **Calling for an "About Us" Date** . . . . . . . . . . . . . . . . . 338
▶ **Talking Without Fighting** . . . . . . . . . . . . . . . . . . . . . . 314
▶ **Resolving Conflict Quickly** . . . . . . . . . . . . . . . . . . . . 322
▶ **Turning Screaming Matches into Conversations** . . 325
▶ **Finding Solutions for Your FB Problems** . . . . . . . . 328

# Calling for an "About Us" Date

## Our Book Club Picks

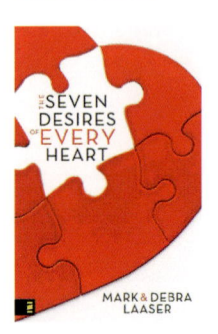

*The Desires of Every Heart* is an instructive and inspirational book by Mark and Debra Laaser who use stories and straightforward observations to examine seven desires we all share, and illustrate how understanding those desires can enhance our relationships and enrich our lives.

**OK, my husband and I need an "About Us" date. How do I bring it up and get him to show up?**

### Jason & Kelli:

Stop stressing about it! Have him read the thread on the "About Us" date. Explain to him how you think it could work for your marriage. Tell him that you think it's a great idea, that a lot of couples do it to keep their marriage healthy, and that you'd like to try it.

### Jason:

You could say something like, "Great things happen in business meetings when people meet on a regular basis with an agenda and a set amount of time. Imagine what could happen for our marriage if we were to do the same kind of thing."

### Kelli:

Or you could tell him you'll make it worth his while to try it a few times. (Wink-wink.)

facebook and Your Marriage

# TMI! Talking with Your Mate Offline About Online Issues

# Calling for an "About Us" Date

**Jason:**

Woohoo! Hey Kel, I think I need some convincing on this "About Us" date.

**Kelli:**

Ha ha. Right, Krafsky. ☺

**Jason & Kelli:**

But the "About Us" dates can't be seen as a dump on your mate session or your personal time to fix your spouse. The "About Us" dates are an opportunity for spouses to connect, to share, to listen and, over time, to strengthen their relationship.

**Jason:**

Give it a trial run for a month. Set up four weekly times, meet, and see what happens. If it works, keep it going. If it's not working, try to figure out why.

**Kelli:**

Some couples have found that combining the "About Us" date with the structure a marriage education program provides (deeper

▶▶▶

## facebook
### and Your Marriage

communication skills, and guidance on topics like finances or intimacy) can help kick start these one-on-one dates into an invaluable part of their marriage experience.

**Jason:**

We have all kinds of links to such programs at **FacebookAndYourMarriage.com**.

## Related Threads:

- ▶ Creative Invites to Date Your Mate . . . . . . . . . . . . 224
- ▶ Resolving Conflict Quickly . . . . . . . . . . . . . . . . . . 322
- ▶ Turning Screaming Matches into Conversations . . 325
- ▶ Uh-Huh is Never Enough . . . . . . . . . . . . . . . . . . . . 331
- ▶ Finding Solutions for Your FB Problems . . . . . . . . 328

**TMI! Talking with Your Mate Offline About Online Issues**

**Creating Your Own Boundaries**

**Off your recommendation, my wife and I agreed to set up some boundaries for our time on Facebook. But we need some help thinking of more than the obvious ones. Is there a list of boundaries somewhere?**

**Jason & Kelli:**

Way to go! You're taking an important step for your spouse, yourself, and your marriage.

Here are 10 questions for each of you to answer on your own, and then get together and talk about your responses. The boundaries you live by as a couple will emerge in the midst of your discussion.

1. How much time each day is an acceptable amount of time to spend on Facebook?

2. Are there times during the week that should be Facebook-free?

3. When accepting Friend Requests from others, who is OK to accept requests from and who is not?

4. Who are the types of people from your past that are OK to search for on Facebook and who are not?

5. How personal can updates and comments get with the sharing of details about yourself, your spouse, your family, your

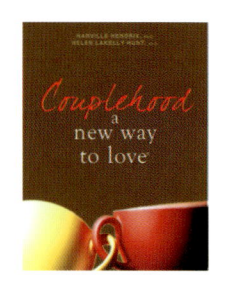

▶▶▶

**Transform Your Relationship**

*Couplehood: A New Way to Love* is a program that helps couples learn the skills necessary to realize their relationship potential. Harville Hendrix and Helen LaKelley Hunt invite couples to consider what their relationship needs from them as individuals rather than what they need individually from their couple relationship.

**facebook**
and Your Marriage

341

work, your life?

6. Are there any words, terms, or phrases that will not be typed and shared publicly?

7. What topics are off limits to write about in updates and comments?

8. Who are the types of FB Friends that are OK to have private communications with using the FB Inbox and Chat feature?

9. What should occur if a FB Friend crosses over the line?

10. How will you and your spouse connect offline about your Facebook experience?

**Jason:**

You really want to take some time to think about these questions on your own before talking them through. In fact, write down your responses to the questions and create your own list of personal and couple boundaries.

**Kelli:**

When you finish making your separate lists, and then discuss and agree on your shared list of boundaries, don't worry if your boundaries are different from other couples. Different couples will have different boundaries because their values, needs, and convictions are, well, different.

**Jason:**

The boundaries you set up will make a tremendous difference in your time as a couple...on and off of Facebook.

## Related Threads:

- Chatting Boundaries........................162
- Friend Requests from Old Flames.............179
- Concerns with Spouse Friending Exes.........242
- Spouse Overreacting on Friend Choices.......284
- Living Inbounds.............................344

# Living Inbounds

# TMI! Talking with Your Mate Offline About Online Issues

## Our Book Club Picks

*Boundaries in Marriage* by Dr. Henry Cloud and Dr. John Townsend helps married people understand the friction point or serious hurts and betrayals in marriage-and move beyond them to the mutual care, respect, affirmation, and intimacy every married couple longs for.

**So my husband and I have our list of boundaries set up. How do we know each other is keeping the boundaries we've set up?**

**Jason & Kelli:**

Congrats on creating the list of your boundaries.

Now test drive them for a few weeks and see if they work. Set up a weekly "About Us" date to see if the boundaries actually work. Are there any issues that have come up the boundaries don't address? If so, create some extras. Are there boundaries that aren't working? Then change them so they meet your needs.

Boundaries are a means to an end. Ultimately, protecting yourselves and your marriage is what matters. If the boundaries are doing their job, keep them. If they're not, drop them and come up with some new ones.

If either of you needs to find greater accountability on your Facebook time (outside the two of you), each of you should find a same-gendered friend or a same-gendered mentor you can individually meet with on a regular basis. This is someone that can be completely trusted to keep things confidential.

## facebook
### and Your Marriage

# TMI! Talking with Your Mate Offline About Online Issues

## Living Inbounds

### Kelli:

In addition to looking out for your best interest, this mentor should also be looking out for the best interest of your marriage.

### Jason:

It could be helpful if this mentor or friend is on Facebook too. Not so they can Facebook about you, but that they understand and can better empathize with the Facebooking culture.

### Jason & Kelli:

In time, the boundaries will be set firmly in place, and you'll hardly notice they're there because they free you to exist and live in a safe place that protects and strengthens your marriage.

## Related Threads:

- ▶ Should Married Facebookers Beware? . . . . . . . . . . 60
- ▶ Creating Your Own Boundaries . . . . . . . . . . . . . . 341
- ▶ The "About Us" Date . . . . . . . . . . . . . . . . . . . . . . 334
- ▶ Go on Facebook Dates . . . . . . . . . . . . . . . . . . . . . 214
- ▶ Finding Help . . . . . . . . . . . . . . . . . . . . . . . . . . . . . 349

facebook
and Your Marriage

# Working Through Infidelity Together

**My husband and I are trying to work through the aftermath of a one-night stand he had with a woman he got to know on Facebook. We're both committed to making our marriage work, but just need some direction on where we go from here. Any help you can provide?**

### Jason & Kelli:

Wow! We applaud you both for standing for your marriage and agreeing to work through the infidelity.

Before healing can begin, what has been done to ensure the affair is over? Has the woman been Blocked from your husband's FB Friends? Has all communication and interaction with her come to a halt? What checks and balances have been set up regarding who your husband interacts with through Facebook and how (public versus private correspondences)?

For both of your sakes, find someone to walk this journey of forgiveness and reconciliation with you (individually and together). A therapist, your clergy, or a ministry or organization that specializes in affair recovery will help ensure you continue down the pathway of healing, even when it gets hard.

### Jason:

At **FacebookAndYourMarriage.com**, we have listed a bunch of incredible resources and organizations that specialize in helping couples overcome and work through what you have experienced.

### Jason & Kelli:

For each of you, give the other what they need — time to process emotions and feelings surrounding the affair, acceptance to be human with handling these feelings, and patience knowing that healing and restoration take time.

As a couple, try to figure out what happened and why. Create new boundaries with Facebook and relationships and set up some sort of accountability system. Find the blind spots, the weak points, and the fragile places in your relationship.

### Kelli:

It may even be a good idea to take a break from Facebook for awhile.

### Jason & Kelli:

Finally, pursue forgiveness. Michele Weiner-Davis, a counselor and author who has worked

▶▶▶

with many couples through infidelity, says to forgive is to make *"a conscious decision to stop blaming, make peace, and start tomorrow with a clean slate."*

■

### Related Threads:

- ▶ Finding Help . . . . . . . . . . . . . . . . . . . . . . . . . . . . . .349
- ▶ Repairing a Marriage I Messed Up . . . . . . . . . . . .308
- ▶ Spouse Wants a Do-Over . . . . . . . . . . . . . . . . . . . . 274
- ▶ Closing Facebook Account . . . . . . . . . . . . . . . . . . 200
- ▶ Hiding, Removing & Blocking People . . . . . . . . . .191

# TMI! Talking with Your Mate Offline About Online Issues

# Finding Help

**My wife and I have both made some mistakes on Facebook that have done some damage to our relationship. We agree that getting some professional help is a next step. Know any good counselors?**

### Jason & Kelli:

It is great to hear when a couple realizes the need for a third party AND acts on that realization. Unfortunately, many couples wait way too long before they reach out for help.

There are several options for you: marriage and family therapists, pastoral counseling, marriage intensives, and marriage organizations that specialize in helping troubled marriages.

**Marriage and family therapists:** Not all counselors specialize in marriage therapy. And unfortunately, not all marriage and family therapists are marriage-friendly. Interview the therapist to make sure you both click with him or her, that you feel comfortable with their philosophy, and that the therapist is committed to strengthen your marriage...regardless.

**Pastoral counseling:** Lots of churches and houses of worship have pastoral counselors on staff. In most cases, they blend counseling practices with elements of faith and theology. Anymore, pastoral care is available to people outside of the congregation, so check out the local church,

## Making a Difference

The Association of Marriage and Family Ministries has a web-based clearinghouse featuring every kind of ministry offering to serve married and unmarried couples and parents.

▶▶▶

**facebook**
*and Your Marriage*

349

parish, or congregation and see if they have services to help your marriage.

**Marriage intensives:** This fairly new concept in therapy is having great success. Rather than dragging marriage issues out over a period of months, couples can meet with a team of trained therapists over the course of a weekend or week for intensive all-day counseling and care. Amazing things can happen in just a few days.

**Marriage education organizations:** All across the country, there are organizations that provide marriage education to couples ranging from skills-based communication classes to weekend retreats. There are a number of organizations whose primary focus is on helping couples who've experienced infidelity or are in troubled marriages. These organizations are run by passionate people and couples devoted to helping bad marriages become better and good marriages become great.

Being in the premarital and marriage education field, we know a number of marriage and family therapists, counseling networks, pastoral care networks, and organizations specializing in helping troubled marriages. At **FacebookAndYourMarriage.com**, we have links to a wide range of networks for all of the possible avenues for help.

**Jason:**

Whatever direction you end up going (therapists, pastoral counseling, intensives or organizations), the important thing is to be tenacious in finding something that will work for you, your spouse, and your marriage.

**Kelli:**

And once you've found the source of help, be prepared to make the changes both of you need to make to move your marriage to a better place. It takes time, but it is so worth it!

## Related Threads:

- ▶ Talking Without Fighting . . . . . . . . . . . . . . . . . . . . . 314
- ▶ Setting Up Boundaries . . . . . . . . . . . . . . . . . . . . . . . 319
- ▶ Finding Solutions for Your FB Problems . . . . . . . 328
- ▶ Creating Your Own Boundaries . . . . . . . . . . . . . . 341
- ▶ Living Inbounds . . . . . . . . . . . . . . . . . . . . . . . . . . . 344

- ▶ Appendix A: Get More from
  *Facebook and Your Marriage* Online .................354
- ▶ Appendix B: Facebook Jargon ......................356
- ▶ Appendix C: Sources...............................360
- ▶ K. Jason & Kelli Krafsky: The Authors ................364
- ▶ Other Books by K. Jason & Kelli Krafsky..............366
- ▶ Order More Copies of
  *Facebook and Your Marriage* ........................370

# Back of the Book Stuff

# Appendix A: Get More from Facebook and Your Marriage Online

**Don't you hate it when you get to the end of the book and you still want more?**

*Facebook and Your Marriage* (the book) and FacebookAndYourMarriage.com (the website) integrate to give you the latest on Facebook and the greatest for your marriage.

Online, find additional information to help you, your spouse, and your marriage, including:

▶ Detailed "how-to" instructions to improve your Facebook experience.

▶ Links to groups and sites that offer advice to further strengthen your marriage..

▶ Lists of more books and organizations aimed at helping your relationship.

▶ Articles and news stories that further expound on *Facebook and Your Marriage*.

▶▶▶

Be sure to join the Facebook Page for *Facebook and Your Marriage* (**facebook.com/FBandYourMarriage**)

If you're on Twitter, follow us at **@FB_and_Marriage** for updates, new links, and more help in your Facebook experience.

View our other marriage strengthening efforts, check out:

**MarriageJunkie.com** — Ramblings of a Marriage Junkie

**FullMarriageExperience.com** — Website for *Before "I Do"*

# Appendix B: Facebook Jargon

**Applications** allow users to access games, quizzes and other special features in their Facebook experience. Some applications are created by Facebook but most are created by third-party companies.

**Block** is when one Facebook user removes another Facebook user as a FB Friend and neither Facebook user will be visible to each other on Facebook.

**Chat** is a feature that allows two FB Friends to conduct a private, real-time exchange by typing short messages to one another.

**Comment** is a way for FB Friends to respond to what another FB Friend has posted, whether it is an update, a picture, a link or anything else.

**Facebook** is an online community that allows people to connect and reconnect with old and new friends, family members, former classmates, and just about anybody else.

**Facebook Friends** or **FB Friends**, are two Facebook users who have mutually agreed to accept each others "friendship" on Facebook which allows for a certain level of accessibility and convenient communications with one another.

▶▶▶

**Friend Lists** allow Facebook users to manage multiple groupings of FB Friends for easier correspondence and determining levels of privacy.

**Friend Requests** are notifications that another Facebook user wishes to connect with you and be your friend on Facebook. You then have the option to "accept" or "ignore" the Friend Request.

**Friend Suggestions** occur due to Facebook's automated system that cross references the FB Friends of a user and searches for common links with other users. The recommendations may or may not be someone the user has ever known or associated with.

**Hide** is an option for Facebook users to remove the posts and updates from a particular FB Friend from their own Home Page, but still keeps the FB Friend and allows for correspondence.

**Home Page** is the place where a Facebook user views the updates and information about all of their FB Friends. The viewing options range from Top News, Recent News, Status Updates, Photos, and more.

**Groups** are user developed groupings meant to foster group discussion around a particular topic area.

**Inbox** or **FB Inbox** is attached to a users account and allows users to send emails to FB Friends and even to people without a Facebook account. While similar to regular email accounts, the Facebook Email is limited in comparison.

**News Feed** is the default view for a Facebook user's Home Page, with two primary views: Top News and Most Recent.

▶▶▶

**Notes** allow Facebook users to capture their own writings and share them with their FB Friends or to upload articles and information from outside of Facebook and file them in the Notes section.

**Pages** provide a space for businesses, organizations, celebrities and brands to broadcast information, and to attract and interact with Facebook users.

**Photo Albums** are a way for a Facebook user to group pictures in user-defined files on Facebook.

**Poke** is a rarely used feature that allows one Facebook user to get the attention of another Facebook user.

**Privacy Settings** are a range of restrictions and protections a Facebook user can customize for their account restricting who can view information, updates, pictures and more.

**Profile Page** is the only page on Facebook that is all about YOU! It contains a picture, your Wall, your Contact Information, your Photo Album, a brief list of your FB Friends, and tabs to help others find more information about you.

**Profile Picture** is the picture Facebook users choose to post on their Profile Page and it becomes the primary image FB Friends see and associate with the user's updates, postings, and comments. The Profile Picture can be changed at any time.

**Publisher Box** is a box located on the Profile Page and the Home Page where a Facebook user can post an update, share a Picture, a Link, a Video, an Event and more.

**Relationship Status** is a Facebook user's way to announce their marital status to others on Facebook.

▶▶▶

**Tag** is when a Facebook user uploads a picture onto Facebook and attaches a FB Friend's name to the photo, ensuring that FB Friend is notified about the photo and has the photo placed on their Wall.

**Unfriend** is when one Facebook user removes another Facebook user as a FB Friend and therefore, both users will no longer see updates from each other.

**Wall** (the Wall) is described by Facebook as "the center of your profile" as it is the opening page on your Profile Page that keeps a record of your Facebook activity including past and current postings, lists of new FB Friends, Pages and Groups that have been joined and more. It is also where FB Friends can leave messages.

# Appendix C: Sources

**Articles:**

"10 Ways To Stay Safe On Facebook," whyfacebook.com. February 6, 2009.

"Baby Boomers Renew Their Connections With Facebook," facebook-news.info. January 29, 2010.

"Don't poke me bro! Facebook 'poke' leads to arrest," YahooTech. October 13, 2009.

"Facebook – The Complete Biography," Mashable. 2007.

"Facebook, Twitter crooks just a click away," Stephanie Chen, CNN.com.

"Facebook's Mark Zuckerberg opens up," CNN.com. July 2009

"Five clues that you are addicted to Facebook," Elizabeth Cohen. CNN.com.

"Husband dumps his wife with online message in 'world's first divorce by Facebook,'" James Tozer. Daily Mail. February 9, 2009

"Latest Data on Facebook's US Growth by Age and Gender," Justin Smith, InsideFacebook.com. November 2, 2009.

▶▶▶

"Nielsen: Facebook Led 2009 Social Media Traffic Growth in the US and Abroad," insidefacebook.com. February 23, 2010.

"Nielsen: Facebook Occupied 7 Hours of the Average US User's January," Eric Eldon, insidefacebook.com. February 16, 2010.

"Our Top Dozen Do's and Don'ts for Facebooking Couples," K. Jason and Kelli Krafsky. marriagejunkie.com. December 2009.

"Past Loves and Facebook: To Connect or Not to Connect," Elisha Goldstein, Ph.D., MentalHelp.net. 2009.

"Social media an inviting target for cybercriminals," Steve Almasy, CNN.com. 2009.

"Study: Facebook users willingly give out data," CNET.com. December 7, 2009.

"The 12 most annoying types of Facebookers," Brandon Griggs, CNN.com.

"The Facebook divorce," Amanda Fortini, Salon.com. September 29, 2009.

"The Power of First Loves," Wendy Atterberry, TheFrisky.com. 2009.

"Twitter Nears Facebook's Daily Status Update Volume," Nick O'Neal, allfacebook.com. February 22, 2010.

"WOW: Facebook Adding Half a Million New Users Every Day," Ben Parr, Mashable.com, November 2009.

"Twitter Hits 50 Million Tweets Per Day," Ben Parr. Mashable.com. February 2010.

## Books/Programs:

*Before "I Do" – Preparing for the Full Marriage Experience*, K. Jason Krafsky. Turn the Tide Resource Group. 2005.

*Boundaries in Marriage*, Henry Cloud and John Townsend. Zondervan. 1999.

*Close Calls: What Adulterers Want You to Know About Protecting Your Marriage*, Dave Carder. Moody Publishers. 2008.

*Facebook Addiction*, Nnamdi Godson Osuagwu, Ice Cream Melts Publishing. 2009.

*Infidelity: A Survival Guide*, Dr. Don-David Lusterman. New Harbinger Publications, 1998.

*Not "Just Friends,"* Shirley P. Glass. The Free Press. 2003

Prevention and Relationship Enhancement Program (PREP) Program, PREP, Inc.

*Private Lies: Infidelity and the Betrayal of Intimacy*, Frank Pittman. W.W. Norton. 1989.

*The Divorce Remedy: The Proven 7-Step Program for Saving Your Marriage*, Michele Weiner-Davis. Simon & Schuster. 2001.

## Sites:

apps.facebook.com/causes/causes?m=17a95901

exchange.causes.com/resources/success-stories/

facebook.com/press/info.php?founderbios

facebook.com/press/info.php?founderbios#!/press/info.php?timeline

facebook.com/press/info.php?statistics#!/press/info.php?statistics

# K. Jason & Kelli Krafsky
## (the authors)

K. Jason and Kelli Krafsky have been married since 1994 and have co-authored *Facebook and Your Marriage*.

Jason and Kelli have co-written three blog articles ("Our Top Dozen Do's and Don'ts for Facebooking Couples," "Is Facebook a Cyber-Threat to Your Marriage?," and "How Facebook Can Improve Your Marriage") that have been widely distributed, written about and reposted.

Jason is also the author *Before "I Do" – Preparing for the Full Marriage Experience*, an interactive premarital book for engaged and seriously dating couples.

For nearly a decade and a half, Jason has worked for organizations whose mission focus is to strengthen the health and well being of marriages and families.

▶▶▶

Jason and Kelli live in the foothills of Washington's Cascade Mountains with their four children.

To invite the Krafskys to speak or for media interviews, contact them through **FacebookAndYourMarriage.com**.

To keep up with the ongoing discussion surrounding *Facebook and Your Marriage*, join the Fan Page at facebook.com/FBandYourMarriage and follow @FB_and_Marriage on Twitter.

Find out more about Jason and Kelli and their other marriage efforts at their website (**FullMarriageExperience.com**) and blog (**MarriageJunkie.com**).

# Other Books by K. Jason Krafsky

## Before "I Do"
### Preparing for The Full Marriage Experience

Recently engaged? Starting to discuss the "M" word with your significant other? Want to get prepared for married life?

Having witnessed countless divorces and relationships that have crashed and burned, many of today's engaged and pre-engaged couples feel some anxiety about their own future marriage.

Will we have a love that lasts a lifetime? Will we be happy? Will we have a marriage that goes the distance?

Turn your "will we" questions into "we will" declarations with, *Before "I Do"- Preparing for the Full Marriage Experience*

▶▶▶

by K. Jason Krafsky. *Before "I Do"* is a fully interactive, dynamic premarital workbook that will prepare your relationship to experience all that marriage has to offer!

Not just another relationship book, *Before "I Do"* guides couples through a series of relationship-building exercises to learn, reflect on, and meaningfully discuss eight relationship essentials.

Topics include: Lay the Foundation for a Lifelong Marriage; Discover God's Gift to You – Your Mate; Fight With Your Mate and Please God Too; Ensure the "I Do's" Last a Lifetime; Walk on the Spiritual Side of Marriage; Prepare the Marriage Bed for a Lifetime of Pleasure, and more.

"The best part of *Before 'I Do'* was how it brought up subjects that we wouldn't have necessarily thought to discuss. We were able to discuss issues, come to agreements and prevent possible future arguments." (M and J)

*Before "I Do"* provides a blend of scriptural principles, relationship skills, and proven insights for engaged and seriously dating couples to live the Full Marriage Experience!

**Coming soon!** New layout and design. Winter 2010.

▶▶▶

Go through *Before "I Do"* on your own, or get more out of *Before "I Do"* by meeting with a pastor, counselor or mentor couple.

Many of the most respected and most influential congregations in America are using *Before "I Do"* for their marriage prep classes, small groups, mentoring and counseling. Seacoast Church, The Moody Church, Canyon Ridge Christian Church, Ginghamsburg Church, First Baptist Church of Woodstock, and hundreds of other churches are using *Before "I Do"*...and loving it!

*Before "I Do"* is also endorsed by leaders of the nation's most respected marriage programs including PREPARE/ENRICH, Christian PREP, Association of Marriage & Family Ministries, Successful Stepfamilies, America's Family Coaches, Georgia Family Council and more!

**Order your His & Hers copies of *Before "I Do"* at FullMarriageExperience.com and save 20%!**

# NEW BOOK!
## Winter 2011 — Watch for it!

### After "I Do"
#### Living The Full Marriage Experience

## Order Form:
# Facebook and Your Marriage

*Facebook and Your Marriage* is full of answers, tips, and hints for how to protect your marriage, enhance your relationship, and deal with the many issues that can come up when you sign in to your profile. And it's presented in a fluid, easy-to-use format that encourages you to follow the threads that most interest you.

Whatever your Facebook experience, you need the practical advice *Facebook and Your Marriage* offers.

### Order online at FacebookAndYourMarriage.com

**Just $19.95 (plus $6.95 S/H) per book**

Washington residents add $2.31 per book to order for 8.6% sales tax

**Mail completed form and payment to:**
Turn the Tide Resource Group
26828 Maple Valley Hwy #260
Maple Valley, WA 98038
Fax: 425.432.1274

**Bulk Quantity & Bookstore Ordering**

**Contact Turn the Tide Resource Group**
Phone: 425.432.8433
T3RG@FullMarriageExperience.com

## Billing:
Name _____
Organization _____
Address _____
City/State _____ Zip Code _____
Phone _____ Email _____

## Shipping: (if different from Billing)
Name _____
Organization _____
Address _____
City/State _____ Zip Code _____
Phone _____ Email _____

## Payment:
☐ I have enclosed a check payable to:
  **Turn the Tide Resource Group**

☐ Please charge my credit card.

## Type of Card:
☐ Visa     ☐ Mastercard
☐ Amex     ☐ Discover

Name on Card _____
Card Number _____
Exp Date _____
Pin _____